SCUNTHORPE
HASTA
LA MUERTE

SCUNTHORPE
HASTA
LA MUERTE

The Extraordinary Journey of
English Football's Spanish Pioneer

Iñigo Gurruchaga

TRANSLATION
Matthew Kennington

deCoubertin
B O O K S

First published in English as a hardback by deCoubertin Books Ltd in 2016.

First Edition.

deCoubertin Books, Studio N, Baltic Creative Campus, Liverpool, L1 OAH.
www.decoubertin.co.uk

ISBN: 978-1-909245-37-2

Cover design by Noah MacMillan.

Translation by Matthew Kennington.

Typeset design and layout by Leslie Priestley.

Printed and bound by Standart.

'Come closer now...
Only you can hear and see,
behind the eyes of the sleepers,
the movements and countries
and mazes and colours
and dismays and rainbows
and tunes and wishes and flight
and fall and despairs
and big seas of their dreams.'

Dylan Thomas
Under Milk Wood

'Once in a lifetime,
a writer is handed on a plate
a gift from heaven.'

CLR James
Beyond The Boundary

FOREWORD BY
XABI ALONSO

The story of Alex Calvo García is not only the journey of a footballer, it is also the tale of adventure into the unknown.

Having played there for Liverpool, I believe England to be the country where the passion of football is lived at its best, be in a team in the Premier League or in the old fourth division.

Clubs, big and small, strive to keep alive their history and traditions through the same energy, passion and commitment.

I remember very well when Alex played in Beasain and Eibar because my father managed both teams when Alex was there. My brother Mikel and myself watched nearly every match. And on Saturday mornings we used to kick the ball and do our own training in the goal left free by the team, testing the reserve goalkeeper.

Alex was always the number 10 in midfield. He had a classy touch that made him noticeable; he had an impressive sense of timing to get into the box and the quality that allowed him to score many 'golazos' (great goals). I recall one of them, in a friendly match of Beasain in Segura. He received the ball from a goal kick without letting it bounce and beat the goalkeeper with a great lob. I wonder whether he still remembers it. I certainly do.

Each footballer's path is different. In the case of Alex, to have played in the old Wembley stadium and to have scored a goal in what for me it has always been the cradle of football, must have been something that cannot be surpassed: a culmination worthy of all the efforts and sacrifice in a person's career.

In a sports world controlled by rapid consumption and cold professionalism, the story of Alex connects us again to the essence of the game of football.

Xabi Alonso, MUNICH, APRIL 2016.

SCUNTHORPE
HASTA LA MUERTE

Football is a game which commences at three o'clock in the afternoon on an English Saturday.

The shutters under the Welcome to Glanford Park sign are lifted, the club employees arrive, later the secretary and the head of security. The Iron bar opens and soon fills with noise, smoke and beer.

The visitors, Yeovil Town, appear, shortly followed by another coach, whose occupants, supporters in white and green striped shirts, stretch their legs after 260 miles on the road by walking around a concrete and steel stadium on the outskirts of a town.

Players come in sports cars, cheered by optimistic car park attendants. Autograph hunters want their signatures.

A new looking Mercedes parks in a VIP bay. His driver opens the boot and helps the passenger to put on his coat.

Jamie McCombe, who according to the local paper, the Evening Telegraph, is on his way to Lincoln City, emerges from the dressing room in shorts. Legs gleaming in liniment. He hands a ticket to a friend.

Wives wait in cars for the kick off reading magazines.

Claret and blue t-shirts, with the words 'Alex Calvo García The legend' or Adiós La legenda printed on them, are sold in the club shop. Legend is 'leyenda' in Spanish but who cares.

It is March 2004. Calvo García has yet to recover from a serious injury. In September he announced that this is his last season as a professional footballer. He is the club's longest serving player.

It is cold, it rains, the wind is up. Scunthorpe United are two weeks without a game due to the snow. Nine players are injured or suspended. Three have been signed from other clubs on one-month loans. United are seventeenth in the fourth division. There are twenty four teams in the league and the bottom two are relegated from professional football. Yeovil rose from the depths below just last year and now they are in seventh place. Seventh will get you into the end of season play-offs.

Football is a game which commences at three o'clock in the afternoon on an English Saturday.

It is an inauspicious start and the Yeovil fans taunt their hosts: who are you? who are you?

Who are we? We are Scunthorpe United. A team whose only purpose in the first few minutes is to lump long high balls to Steve Torpey; in the hope of a flick or a nod falling to a teammate's feet.

This Scunthorpe usually plays through Peter Beagrie, who honed his craft under the tutelage of a Uruguayan coach, Danny Bergara. Bergara settled in England after playing for Mallorca, Seville and Tenerife in Spain, where he met his English wife. Fifteen years after his arrival he became the first foreigner born in a non-English speaking country to manage a professional league club, Rochdale, in 1988. At the beginning of his career, the Luton Town manager, Harry Haslam, had to sign him as a driving assistant to obtain a work permit so that Bergara could take charge of the youth team.

Beagrie was coached by him at Middlesbrough. The Uruguayan could show his players how to kick a ball. According to Alan Biggs in 'The Man from Uruguay', one of his party tricks was to take a coin out of his pocket, drop it, flick it back up with the outside of his heel and land it at the centre of his forehead.

Bergara led Stockport County to promotion, and four times to Wembley. But he left in acrimonious circumstances, falsely accused of punching the owner of the club. The verdict of an industrial tribunal which reviewed the case vindicated him. But the damage to his reputation had been done, as was the case years later with Beagrie, the 'wild man' of Everton. The First Division Everton squad stayed in San Sebastián during a pre-season tour in 1991 after playing against Real Sociedad to commemorate the founding of the Ordizia K.E. club. After a night out drinking, Beagrie had supposedly driven a powerful motorbike through a glass door into the reception of their hotel in Mount Igeldo, overlooking the bay of San Sebastián.

Really, none of this ever happened. After the game in Ordizia, he and some of his team-mates went down the hill to the town. It was during the local fiestas and there was a rock concert on the beach. They befriended some locals who gave them a lift back to the hotel. Beagrie got his trouser leg caught in the bike when he was dismounting and as he tried to find his footing he broke a small decorative glass panel and cut his leg.

Football attracts dodgy owners and celebrity journalism. Beagrie was tainted like his Uruguayan coach by misdeeds committed by others.

He is injured today and Yeovil play with a very tall Portuguese in the centre of defence, Hugo Rodrigues, who deals comfortably with every ball hoofed in his direction. The visitors are faster and seem to follow a better pattern of play.

Scunthorpe field twenty-year-old Cleveland Taylor on the right wing. He is on loan from Bolton. Wandering like some pedestrian lost in the crowd, he occasionally runs into spaces without apparent connection with the game. The ball never reaches him. He turns to the bench looking alarmed as if being shouted at. Nobody has said anything to him. But as the match progresses he moves better, gets the ball more. He attacks his marker with pace, gets to the byline and crosses.

Darren Holloway, rented for a month to bolster the midfield, wants to show that he is a decent player. At 22 he was with Sunderland in the Premiership. He was sold for 1.2 million pounds to Wimbledon, a club moved by its owner to Milton Keynes, a new town missing the football club in the fabric of urban life.

Holloway got lost in his travels. Injuries and red cards. His contract expires in the summer. Now 26, he needs another club and he is busy breaking Yeovil's flow.

Paul Groves is the other mercenary for a month. A few days ago he was player-manager of arch rivals Grimsby Town. He is 37 and cuts his cloth accordingly. He is a trotter. He covers his channel. Mark, block, give. Pace yourself for ninety minutes among younger men, get to the end of the month, take the pay and see if any offer comes to prolong this odd life of the professional footballer.

Holloway and Groves try to impose themselves in the game. But Yeovil are more settled until Rodrigues gets a bloody nose in a clash of heads with Torpey and leaves the pitch. A woman laughs as the man mountain has to kneel before the physiotherapist to be treated.

Scunthorpe score twice and the fans come to life. They round off with chants of 'Scunthorpe!' the surrealistic verses of the England 1998 World Cup song 'Vindaloo', that carries the name of the spicy marinade- 'vinho de alho', vinegar of wine and garlic - which Portuguese sailors took to the island of Goa.

Now the fans turn their attentions to local rivals Hull City, against whom they play next week, making fun of their name, 'Shitty Hull, Shitty Hull.'

Is it still possible that a run of victories and the return to the team of the Spanish legend would revive this moribund end of the season and the persistent dream of promotion?

Scunthorpe have won. The goals have come from headers in the penalty box. Big Rodrigues returns home holding an ice bag against his nose.

At a quarter to six on a Tuesday evening, two supporters coaches leave for York. Men rattle on about football while teenage boys in baseball caps swear to impress the girls on the front seats. There are children and pensioners too.

The coaches pass the holding parks of car factories, power stations and wintry cereal fields until the windows steam up and nothing can be seen. The passengers sleep.

Old English football grounds tend to be found in working class housing estates, but Bootham Crescent, which was once a cricket field, was built in a richer and more agreeable neighbourhood.

The match programme tells the story of how York City avoided liquidation. The club is now owned by a supporters trust but the societal fraternity is failing on the pitch. The team has achieved just one point in the past two months and are in free fall.

It's below freezing. The away stand has a small café selling tea, cold drinks, hamburgers. The queue is fifteen metres long.

'Iron! Iron! Iron!'

A messy start. York City cuts easily through the Scunthorpe defence after six minutes and a forward lobs the ball over goalkeeper Tom Evans. Wayne Graves clears on the goal line with an overhead kick.

After a quarter of an hour, Paul Groves heads home from a corner. Minutes later, the York keeper gets into a muddle with a high ball and clumsily topples a Scunthorpe player. Penalty. Two nil.

After the break, Brian Laws makes substitutions. Jamie McCombe, who is still heading for Lincoln City according to the Telegraph, takes his place at the centre of defence. He slips and pulls his opponent's shirt in his first move. Yellow card. He then tackles a player from behind. Red.

McCombe was once described in a national paper as a player for the future in English football but his farewell from the club that developed him as a youth player is a long slow walk to the dim tunnel. Laws ignores him as he passes the bench. Fans scream obscenities.

Among those shouting their goodbyes at McCombe is a well-dressed man in his sixties with white hair curling at the back. He turns to the youngsters around him looking for their approval after throwing abuse at the various targets of his fury. He shouts, turns, jumps like a happy child and laughs. And then he bends and stretches his legs to combat the cold.

The sending off lifts the home fans and spurs the customary pessimism of the visitors. The London supporters have coined in Latin a motto for their club – Semper Proximus Annus Est: There Is Always Next Year. But the York goalkeeper must also be feeling the cold as he fails again to deal with a corner and Groves scores from inside the six yard box.

'Ten men and three nil up, ten men and three nil up!'

A voice tells us through loudspeakers that 2663 are watching.

At the bottom of John Staff's cap, passing down the aisle of the coach collecting a tip for the driver, small change rattles. The bus traverses the beautifully lit centre of the archiepiscopal city and then most passengers sleep.

Mothers await their sons at Glanford Park. The old coach driver makes his way around the town delivering his waning load. By the time he reaches The Baths Hall it is quarter past eleven and it is drizzling sleet. Those who did not eat earlier now dine on a bag of chips.

More chips and more cold the following evening as Scunthorpe reserves play Boston United reserves. Five or six first team regulars are in the Scunthorpe team but they lose three nil.

Thirty people are watching. They can hear the voices of footballers submerged under the noise of the crowd on match days. 'Give, give, man on, man on'. Beagrie is now 'Beagsy'. Sharp is 'Sharpy'. Hayes, 'Hayesy'.

An engine can occasionally be heard in the freezing night. A train carrying its load to the steelworks.

Alex Calvo García plays his first ninety minutes after five months. When footballers are out for so long they are overcome by the speed of the game. The ball always falls to the feet of the opposition, the out of form player always chasing; lungs on the verge of exploding, muscles crippled with pain.

Calvo García, the legend of Scunthorpe United, runs fast towards the dressing room on the final whistle, as if not wanting to hear the echo of the last train.

The point of departure for the extraordinary travels of Alex Calvo García in English football was a tarmac pitch in a school bearing the name of a great explorer.

On 1 July 1525, at 16 years of age, Andrés de Urdaneta set sail from the port of A Coruña bound for the Spice Islands in the East Indies under the flag of Holy Roman Emperor Carlos V. Captain of the Sancti Spiritus and head pilot of the expedition was Juan Sebastián Elcano, who three years earlier had completed the first circumnavigation of the world.

Still suffering from severe ciguatera poisoning after eating a barracuda while moored off Annobon Island in West Africa, Elcano lost his ship in a storm near the Cape of Eleven Thousand Virgins, after mistaking the estuary of the River Gallegos for the Straits of Magellan.

On board was his young protégé Urdaneta, whose mother tongue was also Basque and who was witness to Elcano's last will before he died.

Urdaneta reached his destination in the only surviving ship after the fleet was ravaged during the six months that it took them to cross the straits. He stayed in the Spice Islands for nine years.

On his return to Spain, he reported to the court and set sail again for Mexico, where he entered into the order of the Augustinians. His growing reputation as a student of navigation and climate caught the attention of King Philip II, who asked him to join a new mission of conquest and evangelization to the Philippines. Miguel López de Legazpi, born in Zumarraga, a short distance from Urdaneta's home in the town of Ordizia, was the commander.

The highlands of Goierri were rich in timber and ironworks. Nails and anchors were made for the shipyards on the Basque coast. From the port of Bayonne, ships contracted by Italian merchants sailed for the Mediterranean. From Pasajes, they parted to the coasts of Greenland, Canada or Iceland to fish whales and cod. Those ports also enjoyed a thriving commerce with England. The trade of coopers, caulkers and spinners flourished. The sons of wealthy families were trained as sailors in the service of the Spanish monarchy.

Urdaneta studied Latin, Philosophy, Mathematics and Astronomy. After his eventful first expedition, he became a cartographer and administrator in remote lands. At nearly sixty years of age, he persuaded the emperor and the viceroy that he was the man to find a passage for the return trip from the Spice Islands to the western coast of Mexico. No crew had ever undertaken such a journey – 7,500 miles – and returned.

Once he had fulfilled his mission, helping with the settlement of the expedition in the Philippines, he embarked from Cebu on the first of June 1565, and after initially heading north to find favourable winds he reached the port of Acapulco in September, opening a route of navigation and commerce in the Pacific Ocean.

Today, manor houses, the old church and public gardens are reminders of Ordizia's past. The crests of the Aralar range can be seen in the horizon. Every Wednesday in the main square a thriving market set the prices of agricultural produce for the region. And the memory of Urdaneta lingers in the name of streets and neighbourhoods. A statue of the cosmographer was erected at the end of the nineteenth century. Two handsome savages sit at the feet of the priest raising his hand to the heavens.

The school named after Urdaneta was built by the side of the Spanish National Road One, running over the tracks of an ancient royal highway linking the Castille plateau with the shores of the Gulf of Biscay in Spain and then into France through the lowlands of the western Pyrenees. The school has a narrow football pitch made out of asphalt, sandwiched between houses, classrooms and a slope rising to the railway lines.

Alex Calvo García was born on 1 January 1972 in his grandmother's house, but lived with his parents and brothers in the high-rise flat known as 'the skyscraper' of Altamira. At the time of its construction, this eight storey building was unique in the area. The neighbourhood was built close to factories and warehouses, separated from the old town by the highway.

The abundance of woods and rivers had made the area favourable for the establishment of ironworks and the mid-nineteenth century saw the arrival of coke furnaces. Iron ore from Biscay was exchanged for coal imported on ships from southern England and Wales.

In 1865, on a rare strip of flat land between Ordizia and Beasain, an iron refinery and smelting plant with three blast furnaces was built. It became the Compañía Auxiliar de Ferrocarriles or CAF during the twentieth century and was dedicated to the construction of locomotives and carriages for the Spanish railways.

Metallurgical workshops and small factories were created. The population of Ordizia, less than one thousand inhabitants in the nineteenth century, had multiplied to ten thousand.

Alex's father, José Miguel Calvo, joined the apprentice school of CAF at fourteen to study metal structures. The factory employed three thousand.

Unhappy about injustices and with the official trade union under the military dictatorship of General Francisco Franco, Calvo joined Comisiones Obreras (Workers Committees), a union linked to the outlawed Communist Party. He had grown a bushy moustache and people nicknamed him 'Zapata' after the Mexican revolutionary. He took part in illegal strikes and was dismissed in 1968.

He had recently married María del Carmen García, who had come with her family to the neighbouring town of Lazkao when she was seven. Tractors had ruined her father's cart business in the southwestern Spanish region of Extremadura. They moved north and her father found work in a forge while her mother laboured the garden of the landlords of the house they rented.

On the 2nd of October 1972, Alex's father was stopped by a Civil Guard road block along with two comrades. They were carrying leaflets to distribute in a nearby village.

'What are those?' asked a guard, who had seen the leaflets on the dashboard of José Miguel's Renault 8.

A woman had seen them in Ordizia and reported it to the Civil Guard, who then went in search of the culprits.

The men were pushed into the back of the police jeep, beaten with the butts of submachine guns and driven to the mountains. The driver stopped in a hamlet and his companions let comrade Cordero out. But he made such a fuss that, if the guards had any intention of shooting him with the excuse that he had tried to escape, they had to change plans. He was pulled back into the jeep and all three were brought to the Civil Guard barracks. As soon as they arrived, comrade Huerta had a molar smashed with the butt of a pistol. It was his first day back from honeymoon.

José Miguel was tied up and whipped with a metallic wire. His collarbone was badly injured and his hands had turned purple from the tightness of his handcuffs. He later woke up in a bathtub, not remembering how he got there.

Mari Carmen had just fed her children, Mikel, who was five, and Jandro, or Alex, who was eight months, when the doorbell rang. It was eleven in the evening. She went down to the ground floor and looking through the window saw a large number of guards waiting outside.

She told the guards that she had left the keys in her flat, went back in the lift and dumped all of her husband's papers on the second floor landing. The guards chief split his men into two groups. Some took the lift with Mari Carmen and the others went up the stairs. The bundle of evidence was found.

They searched for more like a pack of wolves. In the kitchen and the lounge, in the children's bedroom, under the mattress of the cot. Mikel was crying. Jandro wet himself. At 5am the 24-year-old Mari Carmen and her children crossed the highway on foot with Mikel still in his pyjamas. A CAF worker, on his bike going to his shift, saw them. When they reached her in-laws house tears ran. They went to the barracks. 'I would let you in but I can't', a young guard said.

Inside, a corporal of the traffic division in the Civil Guard asked José Miguel what had happened. After an explanation had been given, the guard said: 'This is inhumane'.

The accused were all later taken to headquarters in San Sebastián. After questioning they were transferred to prison. This was the beginning of a tour of Franco's jails. Martutene, Carabanchel, Martutene, Jaén. He was sentenced to two years for illegal propaganda and another two for illegal association. Alex did not see his father until the summer when his mother took him to the prison in Jaén, Andalusia, 490 miles from home.

Parcels began to arrive to the flat in Altamira. Sleeping bags, blankets, women's clothes and a bit of money was sent to them from countries governed by communist parties: Russia, Bulgaria, Yugoslavia. The mother did some sewing to earn a bit of cash. Mikel, the eldest son, went to live with grandparents. José Miguel's friends and workmates had collections to help the family. Mari Carmen received donations from people who had never been involved in the political rebellions of the time. The Catholic church's own charity, Caritas, regularly gave her money until her husband's release.

The communists organised a seven-a-side football tournament among teams of the workers commune in the prison courtyard of Carabanchel. 'Zapata' played in the Basque team, who lost the final 2-1 against the communist prisoners from Madrid.

The father of the Scunthorpe legend was released from prison a few days before Christmas 1975. Franco had just died. The family was together again just as Spain was opening the door to the idea of democracy.

And the boy they call Jandro has a ball, the simplest of toys. At playtime he runs rings around his opponents on the school pitch and after classes he does the same in Altamira.

Next to the housing estate stands the sports stadium, with a grass pitch and athletics track. It has on the side a gravel surface and two goals. 'The Annex', where Alex plays whenever he can.

The talented young footballer from Urdaneta Primary School has his future determined. He dreams of playing for Real Sociedad but he will more likely follow in the footsteps of his father into the CAF factory. Times have changed. 'Zapata' has returned to his job. The unions are free. But more pain and brutality has come in the guise of ETA, an armed group which is strong in Goierri and other Basque regions. It is killing some of its many enemies in the name of a Basque state, independent from both Spain and France.

In June 1982, the school takes its pupils to Loyola to celebrate the end of the academic year. They are going to visit the birthplace of another servant of the Spanish crown. They jump into a coach on route to Azpeitia, where Iñigo Lopez de Oñaz y de Loyola, founder of the Jesuits, was born.

The life of Iñigo, Enecus, Ignatius or Ignacio de Loyola is better known than Urdaneta's. He was educated in the homes of family friends close to the royal court. After being wounded during one of the last battles to unite the crowns of the Iberian peninsula, the young warrior wanted to spend his recovery reading novels about the adventures of gallant knights, but could only find a book on the life of Jesus Christ.

This was the beginning of a revelation which took him to Jerusalem, Paris and Rome. It was in sixteenth century Rome where he founded, under the watchful eye of the Inquisition, a Christian movement that responded, with firm allegiance to the Pope, to the schism of Protestants worried by predestination.

Alex and the young school children traverse the village of Azpeitia. Manor houses of the old nobility crammed in narrow streets and new blocks of flats built to accommodate the families of tinkers, carpenters, printers and labourers.

In Loyola's neighbourhood, below the rocky mass of Mount Izarraitz, the bus moves through a wide avenue flanked by plane trees, pines, magnolias and beeches. At the end of the esplanade rises the baroque basilica built in memory of the saint. The students are shown the coats of arms of the Bourbon and Hapsburg dynasties hung in the dome to demonstrate Iñigo's diplomatic abilities.

They visit the family home and read an inscription telling the story of how Iñigo's mother gave birth to his last son in the stable, just like Jesus. As the youngest of thirteen siblings, Iñigo would listen in awe to his brothers' tales about their adventures in Granada, Naples, Alger, Hungary or America in service of the Spanish Empire.

At the end of the visit, Alex can now believe that the future is unwritten. Iñigo's final choice of crucifix over sword was made by a wandering mule. Espoused to his new faith after reading the lives of Jesus and of saints, he travelled to Montserrat monastery in the Eastern Pyrenees. According to his autobiography, he stopped on his way to talk with a mounted Muslim where they argued about the virginity of Mary. After parting company, Loyola was so livid that he considered pursuing the heretic and killing him. Baffled by the choice of drawing the sword or continuing on his mystical journey, he let go of his mule's reins at a crossroads. The mule chose the holy path.

The pupil from Urdaneta Primary School listens to all this but he has had his own pagan revelation. The bus driver tells the children that after driving them to Loyola he will go to the airport in Bilbao to pick up the England football team. They are arriving that day to take part in the World Cup.

The ten-year-old Alex is amazed and when he is leaving the coach approaches the driver and asks him for a favour.

'Can you give this comic to Kevin Keegan?'

Keegan in 1982 is one of the most famous footballers in the world. The boy from Ordizia has heard about his goals with Liverpool and his move to Hamburg. He has collected the English striker's stickers in his albums and has seen him on television. Kevin Keegan and his flashy perm, copied by the youth of the day, possibly inspired by the hair style of the Sun King, Louis XIV, who had begun work at his Versailles palace on the same day in which the foundation stone for the Basilica of Loyola was laid.

At the same time Alex sent his comic to Kevin Keegan, the famous footballer had pain in his back.

Ron Greenwood, the England manager, and the team doctor rejected Keegan's requests to fly to Germany to be treated by a specialist who had cured him before. National medical pride was at stake. He was given an epidural injection, but this analgesia commonly used to ease childbirth did not solve Keegan's back troubles. He was unable to play in the opening game of the World Cup.

In the end, they allowed him to go to Hamburg, but nobody should know. He left Bilbao for Madrid at midnight, driving a car borrowed from the manager of the hotel. He was back two days later.

The German doctor had adjusted his damaged vertebrae without injections. But Greenwood did not play him in the next game, which was against West Germany.

Keegan was initiated into football by a nun who refereed matches among pupils at St. Francis Xavier Primary School in Balby, a suburb of Doncaster. Francis Xavier had been a follower of Ignatius of Loyola.

The Keegans were miners in the north-east, originally from Ireland. Kevin's grandfather is remembered for his bravery in the Stanley Pit disaster, which took the lives of 168 men. The family later moved to Doncaster.

Kevin grew up in a terrace house with an outside lavatory. The local children would cross the backyard to play ball games around the coffins of a funeral home. The owner had once shown them the corpse of the man with a white beard and a reputation for drinking, who used to earn a few bob at Christmas time at the Co-op. Father Christmas had died.

The boy Kevin wanted to be a goalkeeper. He would make saves in the park between improvised posts made with a tree and the push chair of his little brother. But at his next school, St. Peters, he was told that he was too small to play in goal. He moved forward and became a winger. A doctor had warned him that due to a wheezy chest he would never make a great sportsman. At fourteen he had a trial with Coventry City. He made it to the last two, but at the end of a six week extension was sent back home.

In 1966 he ran fifty miles with other members of a youth club raising money for a charity providing holidays for orphaned children. They were met by the mayor of Doncaster and their pictures were published in the local newspaper.

Keegan says in *My Autobiography* that he used to play on Saturdays for the reserve team of Pegler Brass Works, where he was an apprentice, and also for Elmfield House Youth Club. On Sundays, for the pub team of the Londsdale Hotel, a place he'd never entered as a customer.

One day after a match, he was asked by his marker, Bob Nellis, if he would be interested in a trial at Scunthorpe. They went in Nellis' furniture delivery van.

At the end of the journey he joined a match between the reserves and promising locals in the car park of the Old Showground. The manager of the club, Ron Ashman, offered him an apprenticeship. The wage of four pounds and two shillings a week was almost two pounds less than what he was earning at Pegler. But he wanted to be a footballer.

He got up at six every morning, took two buses and hitch-hiked the remaining twelve miles to Scunthorpe. When he turned sixteen, his pay was increased, in accordance with a national agreement, to seven pounds and a small allowance for accommodation.

Apprentices cleaned and polished the boots of the first team players, painted the turnstiles and the lines on the pitch, cleaned the floodlights and cut the grass. The club physiotherapist used the facilities at the ground for private clients and the players had to wait for a red light to indicate they could enter the room.

'Those were the days when I was closest to the supporters', Keegan wrote thirty years later. 'They could come and tell you what they thought, not aggressively, but taking a real interest. Now, as the game moves away from its roots, it is the executive type of supporter who is given those privileges, the people who pay for hospitality packages rather than the dyed-in-the-wool fans'.

Kevin Keegan made his debut in the Fourth Division against Peterborough. Getting into the first team was a triumph and a relief. It was certainly safer than playing in the Midlands League against the hard men of amateur mining teams. In the 1966/67 season, Scunthorpe finished fourth from bottom and celebrated with a trip to the Costa Brava.

The fifteen pounds a week in winter were reduced to ten in

summer. It was not enough and the players did temporary jobs at the steelworks. Keegan learned plate-laying under the watchful eye of a Ukrainian foreman. He learned as well what unhappy supporters meant and felt when they shouted at players, demanding they be sent to do a real job.

The three official team pictures taken during his time as a Scunthorpe player show facets of the young man, who became one of the most famous footballers in the world. In 1968, he is seated at the end of the front row, fresh and happy faced. In 1969, the photographer departed from the traditional composition of three rows, with some players sat on the ground, others on a bench, and the rest on their feet. All are kneeling and with arms crossed, a creative *faux pas*. Keegan, in the centre of the picture with a Beatles haircut. In 1970, he is standing up at the back; on his tip toes, trying to look taller.

He was small, fast and fearless. After three years in the most modest division of English professional football, Bill Shankly came calling. The Liverpool manager had been informed by Geoff Twentyman, his chief scout, that there was a promising youngster at Scunthorpe. He watched him in an FA Cup tie at Tranmere and bought him in the spring of 1971 for £35,000 pounds. When he took off his shirt during his medical for Liverpool, Shankly said he could have been a boxer. Keegan had spent hours in the room that passed as a gym at the Old Showground or running up and down the stairs of the stands with weights.

Moody and kind, somewhat naïve, the boy from Doncaster found a father figure in Shankly, also a miner's son. He had taken a mediocre club and turned it into one of the best in Europe. Keegan saw him as an austere man, in both life and words. He led by articulating a common cause rather than tactical analysis. Keegan wrote that he rarely instructed him about how to play, but 'gave me my head'. The new boy, who had arrived late for his first match, was simply told:

'Go and enjoy yourself, son'.

Keegan also found in Liverpool a great playing partner.

John Toshack became obsessed with football against the will of his teachers at Canton High School, where the sporting spirit was instilled on rugby fields. But he was an intelligent student. He earned O levels in French and History before signing as an amateur for Cardiff City. His autobiography, 'Tosh', was entirely written by himself, and he has composed and published poems about games and players.

John Charles was his first hero and his team-mate in Cardiff. But after four years at the club and with one hundred goals on his CV, Bill Shankly called. 'He was sharp, keen and alert and gave you the impression that he could see out the back of his head', remembers Toshack. After six months, he was going to play in the FA Cup final and the club had signed another striker. His first impression of him was very good. His wife, Sue, told him that the boy from Scunthorpe had travelled to London with wives, staff and members of the squad who were not going to play at Wembley. And Keegan had carried her case from the train to the coach. Liverpool lost that final to Arsenal, but after the summer the partnership of Toshack-Keegan was born.

The synchrony between them on the pitch was such that a television channel conducted an experiment. Toshack was asked to choose between a range of shapes and colours, and Keegan was asked to see if he could guess these choices. Then the roles were reversed. Keegan guessed one right but Toshack got four out of five, much to the delight of the producers. The Welshman calmed his partner later. He had seen Keegan's picks in the reflection of the camera lens.

Keegan moved on to Hamburg in Germany. His wife spoke German and he also learned it in order to integrate and settle. They returned to England, first to Southampton and later to fulfil a childhood dream at Newcastle United, then in the Second Division. And after retiring in Newcastle United, he moved to Marbella:

sunshine, golf, the quiet life.

He returned again to manage Newcastle, a team on the brink of relegation to the Third Division. In three years they were vying for victory in the First Division. They lost the decisive match to Liverpool at Anfield, where the Kop was now filled with plastic seats.

Keegan became England manager and delighted the fans with his ability to create a dazzling spirit in a team often subsumed in doubts about its own value. But they lost to Germany in the last international game played at the old Wembley stadium. He quit immediately after that defeat against the greatest enemy.

John Toshack left Anfield shortly after his scoring partner. Diminished by his chronic injury, he went back to South Wales as player-manager of Swansea City and took them from the Fourth Division to the First in four years. It was the beginning of a long trip by this sun worshipper, managing clubs as big as Real Madrid and as small as Khazar Lankaran. He has worked in Portugal, Spain, France, Italy, Macedonia, Azerbaijan, Morocco. At an early stage in his itinerary, he stopped in San Sebastián to take charge of Real Sociedad.

Football reached Spain in the late nineteenth century in the hands and feet of students returning from England, of employees of British companies in mines or shipyards and teachers in Irish schools. A political movement by the name of Regenerationism encouraged sport as part of its ambition to halt the country's decline. They wanted rejuvenation and athletic effort was one of their remedies. The Bourbon monarchy also enjoyed sport.

In San Sebastián players enrolled in the local cycling club and, after winning the first ever Spanish cup, they formed their own, la 'Sociedad de Football', which received the royal seal of Alfonso XII and became Real Sociedad.

There was a notable presence of British players. The first game against Athletic, from Bilbao, was held on 7 November, 1909, and was won by the team from San Sebastián, with McGuinness playing as a forward. Crawford was the Athletic goalkeeper. A month later, a combination team made up of Athletic and Real players beat a selection of foreigners from both clubs 3-0.

In the French Basque country, rugby was more popular, spread by British merchants in the wine regions of the south west of France and school teachers. But football took strong roots amongst the young in the Spanish Basque country.

The first Liga was disputed in 1928 by the various Cup winners – four Basque teams (Athletic, Arenas, Real Sociedad and Real Unión) as well as Barcelona and Real Madrid-, the three runners up of the Cup – Español and Europa, both from Barcelona, and Atlético de Madrid-, and Racing de Santander, who had won a qualifying tournament.

Athletic was the best team in the early years. They were frequent cup winners and won La Liga four times between 1929 and 1936, but clubs in smaller Basque towns lost their rank after the introduction of professionalism.

'At the international level sport is frankly mimic warfare,' wrote George Orwell in *The Sporting Spirit*. ' But the significant thing is not the behaviour of the players but the attitude of the spectators: and, behind the spectators, of the nations who work themselves into furies over these absurd contests, and seriously believe — at any rate for short periods — that running, jumping and kicking a ball are tests of national virtue.'

Orwell wrote *The Sporting Spirit* in 1945, after a tour of England by Dynamo Moscow. It is a short essay where the Eton pupil, International Brigadista in the Spanish Civil War and author of *1984* showed his contempt for the passions of football, which have had political overtones in the Basque Country.

The Basques have preserved an ancient language that is at the root of their strong sense of identity. During the Civil War in the thirties, an autonomous Basque Government was formed and it created a football national team with players from Athletic, Real Sociedad and other Basque clubs. The Euzkadi squad toured Europe and Latin America, competed in the Mexican league. Its players dispersed into Latin American clubs or returned to Spain after the war.

Britain had received more than three thousand children evacuated from Bilbao when General Franco's nationalist troops were approaching the city. They arrived to Southampton in 1937 and among them were Emilio Aldecoa, who played for Wolverhampton Wanderers and Coventry, and also Sabino Barinaga and Raimundo Pérez Lezama who joined Southampton. After their return, Aldecoa and Lezama, both goalkeepers, were capped by Spain. Barinaga went from Southampton to Real Madrid, and after retiring as a player he had a long career as manager of Spanish and Mexican clubs and of the national teams of Nigeria and Morocco. Aldecoa returned briefly to England in 1960 to be assistant manager at Birmingham City.

The Gallego brothers, José and Antonio, did not return to their country after the war. After settling in a hostel for war orphans in Cambridge, both played for United. The elder brother, José, an 'outside forward', moved to Brentford and then to Southampton in the Second Division. Antonio played in goal in only one match for Norwich City, in the first season after the Second World War of what was then the Third Division South.

The new Spanish government revoked the autonomy of the Basque region and their sympathetic newspapers scorned manifestations of local pride. The cover of the first issue of *Marca*, in 1938, a newspaper devoted to sports news, was an image of a young blond giving a fascist salute. Inside the paper, under the headline 'Arm raised to the athletes of Spain', Bilbao born Jacinto Miquelarena wrote: 'In the time of the Republic, football was a red orgy of the smallest regional passions and of the vilest. I did say it with clarity. Almost everyone was separatist and rude watching a game of the Spanish Cup. Basqueist sentiment was present both in the terraces at San Mamés and in the stand of Chamartín (Real Madrid's ground). In most cases the Madrid supporter was a Basqueist from Madrid, a localist, a moron when confronted with the nation limits.'

It is not strange therefore that identification with Athletic, which still advocates a philosophy of signing only Basque players, and Real Sociedad, also had political overtones.

Real Sociedad, San Sebastián's local passion, earned the nickname of 'The Elevator Team' in the post-war period due to the frequency of promotions and relegations between the first and second division. Their fame in those years is due to the introduction, by their coach Benito Díaz, of Herbert Chapman's WM, first played by Arsenal. After a decade in the Primera division, Real went down again in 1962 with a team of locals with some reinforcements loaned by Real Madrid. It wasn't until 1967 that they won promotion.

They returned to the Primera División with a new policy. The team should be a representation of its province, Gipuzkoa. Instead of buying players on the market, they welcomed back veterans who had moved away in their youth to richer clubs. In 1957 Real founded Sanse, dedicated to training youngsters from the region for the first team.

Survival in the Primera depended on the wisdom of one of their best players in the 1920s and 1930s. Amadeo Labarta was the groundsman at their Atotxa stadium. He prepared the turf and had his home at the ground. If the climatic circumstances so required, he poured enough water on the pitch to dampen the filigrees of teams coming north from the drier regions of Spain. Thus 'la Real' discovered through the travails of its academy and the management of the hose a new football identity in white and blue, a tribal empathy of people with the complicity of rain.

Real Sociedad was seen in the 1970s by rival supporters as an ultra defensive team on their away games. They were accused of being obstinate on the tactics of Benito Díaz, who, in addition to Chapman's system, also imported from Switzerland the defensive 'verrou', the barrier. With a packed defence, the occasional talent of a home footballer and the exploits of a prodigal son like Fernando Ansola, one of the greatest headers of the ball in the history of Spanish football, 'la Real' erased the stigma of being a yo-yo team and even played in the UEFA Cup. In their second international experience, Atotxa welcomed the Liverpool of Kevin Keegan and John Toshack. They lost. But making his debut in goal that day was Luis Arconada, the most capped in the club's history.

According to the prevailing theory, the reason for the fertility of the province of Gipuzkoa to produce good goalkeepers was not their youth system, but the local beaches. Children would learn how to stretch themselves to get the ball and to cushion a fall on the sands of the coastline. But there are plenty of beaches in other parts of Spain too.

For whatever reason Real Sociedad became a crib of fine goalkeepers and selling them to other teams helped the club to balance the books. In 1980, when Alex Calvo García was kicking his first balls in the playground of the Urdaneta primary school, the three goalkeepers in the Spanish national team competing in the European Championship finals in Italy, José Antonio González Urrutikoetxea, Peio Artola and Luis Arconada were all products of Real Sociedad. The same three had also defended the goal of another club in San Sebastián, Lengokoak.

In that season 'la Real' finished runners up after staying unbeaten until the penultimate match in Seville. A misplaced pass by one of the survivors of the decade of the water hose, Agustín Aranzabal, known as 'Gaztelu', ended at the feet of Daniel Bertoni, who had won the dictators' World Cup with Argentina. His shot beat Arconada. The title went to Real Madrid. Real Sociedad had not won a national competition since the distant victory of the pioneers of the Cycling Club in the 1909 Cup.

But they won the Spanish league in the next two seasons. Alex was taking his first steps in youth football at a time when his home team was beating the world's richest clubs with the best players available from the small province.

The chant of 'Indians out!' as a protest against the importation by rival clubs of South American players with false documents to claim Spanish ancestry and the policy of recruiting only in the Basque region, earned Real and Athletic a reputation for racism. The exaltations about identity led some players to camouflage their Spanish surnames, but the policy of Real Sociedad at the time was not based in genes but in a requirement to have been raised as a footballer in its catchment area.

Diego, a tireless right midfielder of La Liga winning Real teams, had Spanish surnames: Álvarez Álvarez. He was born in Monforte, in the Galician province of Lugo, but had trained as a youth in Eibar, where his family had migrated. But Roberto López Ufarte used his two Spanish surnames. He was born in the Moroccan city of Fez but grew up in Irun, from where he rose to Real after starring in an international youth tournament in Monaco, where he acquired a French nickname that would follow him throughout his career, 'Le Petit Diable'.

López Ufarte was a rare breed at Real Sociedad, which had established themselves in the first division with a tight defence away from home and by imposing their physical energy in the wet afternoons in Atotxa. Small and fragile, the child prodigy who had outsmarted the invented borders of Africa and Europe dribbled his markers with light touches of the ball on the toe of his boot and sudden movements to throw them off balance. He was a unique artist, the little devil, in a team based on the principle that everyone would take his share of work in a sporting society of equals.

That team of players gathered in a region of four hundred thousand inhabitants reached the semi-finals of the European Cup in 1983. After removing Vikingur of Iceland, Celtic Glasgow and Sporting Lisbon, they drew at home against Hamburg. In Wolksparkstadion, they were eliminated after conceding a goal in the last minute from Thomas von Heesen in an offside position. Hamburg won the final against Juventus.

Twenty years later, in one of his columns published in *El Diario Vasco*, the coach of that time, Alberto Ormaechea, who had been a skilful and hard defender in the era of the watering hose, recalled that game: 'The truth is that they were better than us in Atotxa, although we managed to draw, and in the second leg, the late goal was very controversial. No one will convince me that UEFA were not keener on them playing the final. We were unknowns.'

The fans in Atotxa were now accustomed to winning. The club was enjoying the life of the nouveau rich. Ormaechea was fired as coach after winning two leagues and was replaced by the Welshman John Toshack. He was the first foreign coach of Real Sociedad since the Hungarian Lippo Hertzka had stayed in the city after playing with the German side Essener Turnebund in a friendly match in 1923, at the birth of professional football in Spain.

Toshack's prowess as player-manager of Swansea spread his fame throughout Europe. After a brief spell with Sporting Lisbon, he was hired by the team from San Sebastián. He arrived in the summer of 1985 and immediately displayed his political clout. 'I am a Basque from Wales,' he proclaimed on arrival.

The Welsh bard was versed in language and politics. During his stay in Spain he caused rancorous misunderstandings or hilarity by his insistence in translating literally into Spanish some English idioms: like 'water off a duck's back' or 'pigs flying'. But he dealt with the questions of identity among Basques in the same diplomatic way that he had displayed in Swansea after wearing the red shirt of Liverpool when his team of swans played in Anfield after the death of his mentor and friend Bill Shankly.

Toshack's Real Sociedad combined some of the players who had won the Spanish Liga and a new generation from the academy who would later move to big clubs, particularly to Johan Cruyff's Barcelona, in the new economy of football. His first spell with La Real was happy. He reacquainted himself with Cruyff and others to whom he had met as Liverpool striker. His team won the Copa del Rey, a first since 1909. He went to coach Real Madrid and returned several times to Real Sociedad. When he left San Sebastián for the first time, he was replaced by a former left winger of the club, Marco Antonio Boronat.

Under his rule, in the summer of 1989, the club signed John Aldridge from Liverpool, their first foreign player in thirty years. This new policy did go through a period of obvious racism in the charged political atmosphere of that time. After the arrival of Aldridge, Real recruited English, Swedes or Argentines, but no Spaniard without previous connection with the Basque Country was signed until the arrival in 2002 of Sergio Boris, an Asturian playing with Oviedo.

Aldridge was 31 when he arrived in San Sebastián after suffering a footballing injustice and a moral crisis in Liverpool. Although he was a persistent goal scorer, he was sold when Ian Rush returned abruptly after one season at Juventus.

Three months before, he had lost his faith in football. On 15 April 1989, he played in the FA Cup semi-final at Hillsborough Stadium where 96 fans were crushed to death in the stand.

'I couldn't cope', he wrote ten years later. 'It weakened me physically, emotionally and mentally. The thought of training never entered my head. I remember trying to go jogging, but I couldn't run. There was a time when I wondered if I would ever muster the strength to play. I seriously considered retirement. I was learning about what was relevant in life. I didn't really see the point in football.'

He wanted to stay at Liverpool, but the club which he had followed since he was a boy and which had stirred in him such emotions in recent times, sold him and he felt insulted when talking to directors about a pay-off. Real Sociedad had offered him 'big money', and he went.

In his autobiography, *My Story*, published in 1999, Aldridge wrote about the difficulties he faced as the first foreign player at the club in a generation. When he arrives and sees the bay, he writes: 'It was one of the most impressive sights I've seen.' But Toshack, who had moved to Real Madrid, gave him some advice on 'how to handle the press, how to live in the town from a political perspective.'

The challenges were evident. Aldridge remembers a message painted in the Zubieta training facilities saying 'No foreigners'. The president of a supporters association tells him: 'I'd rather see us in the Tercera División than a foreigner wearing the club's shirt.' He wonders if a man who spits on the ground after calling him- 'Aldrigger!'- is a Basque separatist.

He made friends in the dressing room but also found the isolation of being an immigrant: 'It was inevitable that I should be the victim of the players' jokes. I knew they were laughing at me but, as I couldn't speak Spanish, I had no way of dealing with it. It is probably like that at every club throughout the world. I had to grin and bear it.'

Nationality and football were issues with which John Aldridge was familiar. His ability to find inhabited spaces in the penalty box and his accurate shooting took him to the Irish team of Jack Charlton, a great recruiter of players with Irish ancestry. The taller of the Charlton brothers, who played in the victorious England team of the 1966 World

Cup, brought together an amalgam of recent and distant natives attuned to basic and direct football that overwhelmed opponents with better pedigree.

Aldridge was able to play for Ireland after presenting the birth and marriage certificates of his great-grandmother. In 1996 the European Union of Football Associations demanded that Aldridge and two other players from Jack Charlton's heraldic squad should travel to international competitions using Irish passports, which were issued by the authorities in Dublin. Until then he had used his British papers.

In his first season at Real Sociedad, a club which only a few years before had gone to court against clubs who imported fake Spaniards, John Aldridge suffered food poisoning and his children spend days at home watching British television. When he returns to San Sebastián after his first season, Real have signed Kevin Richardson and Dalian Atkinson. Aldridge understands the difficulties that Atkinson encounters in a city where black skins are exotic. It is not a good season and people are critical with 'the English', who have a reputation for drinking. In the spring of 1991 he picks up his daughter, Joanne, at school and overhears a girl say: 'Joanne is stupid! Joanne is stupid!' Then and there, he takes the decision to return to England, one year before the end of his contract.

In the summer of 1989, when Real Sociedad of San Sebastián sign John Aldridge to revive the ambitions which were once provided by the home boys, Alex Calvo García, 17 years old, joins the youth team. He is known by family and team-mates as Jandro.

The head coach of Real Sociedad academy, Javier Expósito, watches Jandro play for the first time in 1989 on a Sunday morning at Cuatro Vientos, the ground of Sporting Herrera, on the outskirts of San Sebastián. A scout has pointed him towards the youngster from Ordizia.

When assessing a young player, he looks for strength, stamina and whether he is a footballer. If he reacts as if an eel is swirling around his feet when he gets the ball Expósito is not interested. The footballer has to be calm and composed. He believes that you are born a professional footballer and that his mission is to polish the players' skills. A born footballer is resilient and competitive, he displays the same attitude in front of ten spectators or a crowd of fifty thousand.

He watches Jandro. He is the best on the pitch and a footballer. The director of Real Sociedad academy meets him and his father later at his office. He tells them that getting into the academy is the easy part. Now comes the difficult challenge, to play in La Liga with the first team. The young player should be aware that he could be sent home. Therefore he would have to finish his studies.

Expósito was born in Añorga, a neighbourhood of San Sebastián dominated by a cement factory, which built a church, a football ground and a 'Basque pelota' court as part of his social commitment to an area where roofs were covered with grey cement dust. He coached the best footballers in the region while continuing to work in the factory's laboratory.

Jandro is studying boilermaking at the Goierri technical college and that creates a problem. The club gives board and lodgings to their young recruits in a guest house in the capital, but there are no colleges in San Sebastián teaching boilermaking. Jandro will have to stay with his family in Ordizia and travel every day to the club's training facilities.

Expósito raises one last point about the culture of his academy. Long hair is not the style of 'la Real' players. When Jandro returns home he goes for a haircut.

But his qualities do not persuade the coach of the under-19 team, Carmelo Amas, who made his name as a technically gifted right footed winger for Espanyol before finishing his career with Real Sociedad. Jandro cannot break into the first eleven and feels frustrated by being played wide. At the end of the season, Jandro and his father receive another call from Expósito.

He had played some good games but in a football academy there are circumstances which can go against you. Youth players are prepared for certain positions. One year you get six good players vying for the same role and other years you have no one. He should not take this as failure. But Real Sociedad's door is closed for now. The club will loan him to another team and will follow his progress.

Parents expressing their frustration when coaches do not appreciate the wondrous skills in their star child can be troublesome. Fathers who reveal themselves as master tacticians abound in the stands. A tired coach of youth teams in the province of Gipuzkoa delivers in few words his feelings: 'It would be great to be in charge of a team of orphans!' Calvo father and son give Expósito no trouble. The coach remembers the father as a polite and respectful man and his son as a boy with a good head on his shoulders.

Where does Jandro want to go on loan? The club would like him to play in the third division, but he wants to go back to Ordizia, competing in a regional league. It is the summer of 1990, he is eighteen and if he is lucky he could have a long career as an employee in the CAF plant.

Tomás Bosque had been his coach in Ordizia. He had accompanied Jandro and his father on interviews with Expósito and watched all his games; and after each match he had taken him to his home to have dinner and talk about football.

He was also responsible for finding a miraculous healer when a sprained ankle put in doubt Jandro's first visit to Real's academy. Bosque had been told that it could be painful but both of them were unprepared for what was about to occur. They waited in a crowded room on the third floor of a nondescript block of flats, hearing screams from behind a door. They were greeted with a firm handshake by a small man. He twisted Jandro's ankle. Screams. Bosque panicked. Could he still rescue his golden boy? Jandro walked out of the flat without crutches and played his trial match.

Bosque is now in charge of Ordizia's first team and Jandro has become just another number in the lower reaches of football. It hits him hard.

The coach wants him to become the leader of team, the star of Altamira stadium. It has a gate with a modernist feel and gardening features on the slopes around the pitch, planted hedgerows to mark the boundary with the athletics track and a nicely rustic judges' bench at the finish line. It is much better than the old Arana ground, built by supporters moving earth and uprooting trees to create a pitch in the centre of town. The club had been in the third division and one season hosted a Barcelona team in the national amateur championship.

All this happened long ago, at a time when the coach, Celestino Lasa, would take home the leather and lace balls two days before the match placing them in a pot of water heated by firewood; a present for the more gifted visiting players to enjoy their flowery dribbling with a ball like lead in a field of mud.

In the late twentieth century, two hundred people bother to watch their games in Altamira. Everything has changed. Football is not the only game. Few children attend matches in Ordizia daydreaming of being called by the tannoy at the last minute because a player has not arrived; and then he, Jandro, scores the winner, to be the new hero of the town. He is now grown up and plays to a very small crowd in a stadium where coaches, players and spectators complain on cold days about how the delicate architect of Altamira built the main stand facing north, casting a shadow on the pitch causing occasional freezing.

Jandro wants to quit football. Life is shit. Some days he does not go to training and Bosque is told that his silhouette has been seen in the dark areas at the back of the skyscraper. One weekend he goes to Benidorm with his girlfriend. Bosque drops him from the team. He has explained a thousand times that the dressing room is a society of equals.

Bosque has a word with his friend Alfredo del Castillo, with whom he attended coaching courses while they worked at the national telephone company. Del Castillo offers Jandro a contract with Beasain, just promoted to the third division. Jandro crosses the two miles from Altamira to Loinaz, where he finds a football nut case.

Del Castillo was born in Icod, on the island of Tenerife, and got interested in the game when a team from another island in the Canaries, Unión Deportiva Las Palmas, were delighting Spaniards with their brand of football. People talked about a Canarian school reflecting the idiosyncrasy of the islands; a certain slowness, sunshine in the soul. Or it could be the consequence of playing on hard surfaces, requiring control and touch.

Del Castillo learned to play on the streets of Icod with hand crafted balls. A stone, more or less round, had to be found, then well wrapped with paper. Full length women's tights had to be requisitioned to cushion the sphere. And to finish, the ball would be bound with rope.

Stopping those artefacts was his task. He was fast between the sticks and did not mind diving on gravel at a time when goalkeepers did not have gloves or wore knee pads and shorts padded at the hips; and they had to take out small pieces of gravel embedded in the skin after a great save.

Del Castillo may have been too small to be a professional goalkeeper. And when he got a place with the state owned Telefónica, he was randomly assigned to San Sebastián. He landed with tears in his eyes, travelling from Bilbao to his destination in a wooden train creaking at every curve, sitting in front of two men speaking the impenetrable Basque language.

Two employees of the company, who were from Azpeitia, birthplace of Iñigo of Loyola, recommended him to the team of their town, Lagun Onak, meaning 'good friends'. The football crazy Canary Islander took charge of the youth teams before becoming first team coach in the top regional division. Promotion to the third national division was achieved immediately.

He was called by Beasain, which after its founding in 1920 played in a field given to them by the CAF train factory. The club was resigned to signing players rejected by Real Sociedad to complete a squad of locals. But they pioneered the introduction in the lower divisions of new contracts to attract players. They were offered a basic pay to which performance and results bonuses were added.

Alfredo Del Castillo has created an ambitious group and now he has Jandro. In his eyes, his new signing is a complete footballer. He can use the ball well with both feet and, considering his height, is pretty good in the air. There are members of the team with bigger reputations, such as Iñaki Ibañez, who had been in all the divisions of professional football, or Luis Martín Suquía, who played with Real Sociedad. But Jandro is a versatile athlete who can perform in many positions and is conscientious in everything he does.

He is now working in CAF. He draws templates for parts and after work he studies draughtsmanship. When the town's big employer offers him a permanent contract, Jandro refuses. His friends think that he is mad. But he wants to be a footballer.

Del Castillo's Beasain wins promotion to the Segunda División B in 1992. In a team with a 3-3-3-1 formation, Jandro plays behind the striker. He is not a centre forward yet he scores goals and is clever with the ball. He wins the trophy for the most consistent player. It confirms what Del Castillo's old friend Tomás Bosque already knew. Jandro only grows as a player when he feels loved and important, but becomes disillusioned if he is not a protagonist.

It is the beginning of a good period for Beasain. But neither Del Castillo nor Jandro stay for long. The club relegates the coach to assistant of Perico Alonso, who is taking his first steps in management. The father of Xabi and Mikel, who later played in England, was himself a powerful engine in the midfield of the Real Sociedad's team that won two Liga titles before moving to Barcelona.

Eibar offer Jandro a contract to play in the Segunda División. The newspaper *El Correo* publishes a quick fire interview to introduce him to the fans. Hobbies and interests? Football. Favourite food? Pasta. Drink? Water. Movie? Schindler's List. Solo artist? Sting. Group? Almost all. Actress? Jodie Foster. Actor? Jack Nicholson. Players? Stoichkov, Laudrup and Bakero. Problems in society? Unemployment, drugs, corruption and military service. What three things would you take to a desert island? Girlfriend, friends and a boat. Dream? To play every Sunday with Eibar and speak Basque.

Embedded in a narrow valley, with a population of less than thirty thousand, Eibar is proud of its capacity to overcome the challenges of a difficult terrain. Arms factories were established in the nineteenth century, damascene craftsmanship in the region reaching international fame. The UGT workers union created in Eibar, in 1920, the first industrial co-operative of Spain, Alfa, dedicated to the manufacture of sewing machines.

It is a town that tests the boundaries with gusto; the first to proclaim the Spanish Republic in 1931, and also the first in which there was a socialist rally with future president Felipe González as a speaker during the embryonic stages of democracy in the late seventies.

The football club had about three thousand members and an average gate of seventeen hundred people. They had no grass pitch for training and with two first division teams, Athletic and Real Sociedad, within a radius of fifty miles, they settled in the second division, competing against much wealthier clubs. It also had a reserve team, two under 18's, two under 16's, two under 14's, a football academy and three women's teams. No major sponsors and no debts either.

A group of supporters took the reins of the club in the 1980s and nurtured its growth with a new philosophy. They were to become a springboard for aspiring footballers. They would make less money but would be paid at the end of each month, playing for a club traversing Spain by bus, having a roadside sandwich even when travelling to meet the likes of Atlético Madrid.

The club had a salary scale without significant difference between the best and the worst, encouraging their players to follow the example of team-mates like José Ignacio Garmendia, goalkeeper for nineteen seasons while continuing to work at his family's butchers shop.

Jandro's Eibar is coached by José Mari Araquistain, a tall, thin winger who played for Real Sociedad. He is not enamoured by the new signing and he does not play him in the first fourteen games. His debut comes as a substitute in the final minutes of a game against Osasuna in Pamplona on 14 December, 1994, which at 2-0 down seems lost. Alex scores two goals, in the 87th and 92nd minute, causing delirium with the Bombonera.

Despite taking its name from the fans of Boca Juniors in Buenos Aires, the origins of the Bombonera group are English. It all started in the summer of 1982, at the same time as Jandro sent his comic to Kevin Keegan. Supporters of Eibar went to San Mamés stadium in Bilbao to watch the first match of the World Cup between England and France. They liked the songs and mood of the England fans and returned to Eibar with a Union Jack given to them by a spectator in the stand. Eibar's Union Jack had its first airing the day the team won promotion in Durango.

They chartered three planes and a ship during the Easter holiday to support their team in Mallorca, and three trains to accompany the claret and blues in a Cup game against Real Sociedad. The Alfa co-op

SCUNTHORPE HASTA LA MUERTE

wove a banner thirty by fifteen metres to replace the old and tattered Union Jack brought by the founders from Bilbao. The crowds at home games cheered their team with English chants: 'We are Eibar, sha, la, la, la, la', 'Eibarpool, Eibarpool, Eibarpool'.

The 'Bombonera' fans recognise the Ordizia man's goal scoring ability but rarely see him play. In the following season, Perico Alonso is at the helm. Alex plays in every game but never the full ninety minutes. He is downhearted.

Eibar do not offer him a new contract and no other professional club calls.

It is the summer of 1996 and Alex is unemployed.

It is Saturday noon. Three hours to the game, and the Scunthorpe team bus is still parked outside the club offices at Glanford Park.

'It's unprofessional,' Paul complains, huddling from the cold wind and light rain by the porch of the closed club shop. 'It's only thirty minutes to Hull but they could travel in the morning, have something to eat, and go to the stadium in a different way.'

Paul has been following Scunthorpe for thirty-three years. He saw Keegan play. And others.

'Elliott.'

Who played with Leicester City in the Premier League.

'Cox.'

'Where does he play now?'

'At Watford, I think.'

There will be no promotion this year and the team is stuck in one of the deepest depressions of the last twenty years.

'The board has to decide whether to give money to Laws or fire him. Sometimes it seems that they are happy with this.'

Following Scunthorpe is expensive. Paul paid £380 for two season tickets for himself and his son. The coach to Hull is £6 plus £18 for a ticket. The club does not seem to care for the loyalty of people like Paul, who organises his holidays around the team's fixtures. Last year for example, when he was on holiday in Tenerife, he was unable to book a ticket over the phone with his credit card for a cup game at home against Leeds.

He is fed up.

'Maybe next year I'll follow Sheffield United or Hull City. But I've been thinking about it for some time and never do. Following Scunthorpe is like smoking. You want to quit every year but you never do.'

The team bus finally leaves, and twelve more arrive at Glanford Park to take the supporters on the short trip to Hull.

The cavalcade moves onto the motorway, crossing the bridge over the Humber estuary and ventures into enemy territory, Kingston-upon-Hull, a town of about three hundred thousand inhabitants, sprawled around its port.

Police on motorcycles and in cars are waiting at the other end of the bridge to escort the Iron fans. The police cars block any access to the dual carriageway while the motorbikes flank the convoy.

The coaches are parked together outside the stadium and the fans move toward the turnstiles between policemen equipped with riot gear and others on horses.

The one thousand five hundred away fans make their presence known as soon as they enter the away stand with a derogatory chant.

'Who are you? Who are you?'

In the east part of the away end there is a section of empty seats cordoned by stewards to create a corridor between rival fans.

In the west side the separation is less than ten metres. A boy of about twelve stands up and waves his hand in the air accusing the Hull City fans of persistent masturbation. The PA blasts out the strained voice of Paul Weller singing 'A Town Called Malice'.

In the upper tier of a home stand youths mask themselves behind their amber and black Hull scarves.

A man of about forty, with a ridiculous hairstyle and a moustache that fails to camouflage his chubby face, looks towards the visitors with hard and unnerving eyes. Beside him sits a girl, possibly his daughter.

The fans heat up the atmosphere. The choirs - 'Come on Hull! Come on Hull! United! United!' - now interfere with the mystical lyricism of Coldplay.

The stands fill up in the last moment, roaring when the teams take to the field. A fan runs onto the pitch and is taken away by two stewards with orange jackets.

The Hull fans sing their songs. The Iron fans seem to be subdued and perhaps discouraged by the progress of the team, failing to sing on this Saturday one of their most heartfelt compositions.

When I was younger,
I asked my mother,
What should I be?
Should I be Scunthorpe, should I be Hull,
Here's what she said to me ...

Wash your mouth out son,
And fetch your father's gun,
And shoot some City scum,
Shoot some City scum ...

The teams line up. Balls used in the warm up are removed. The referee and linesmen take their positions. A whistle signals kickoff. The mass roars again.

Football is a game which commences at three o'clock in the afternoon on an English Saturday.

Hull start the game with a big boot up field, which is collected by Scunthorpe goalkeeper Tommy Evans.

Is there any cabalistic reasoning into why you would gift possession to your rival in the first move of the match?

The Scunthorpe fans do not like Hull.

'Shitty hole! Shitty hole!'

Now they sing 'Always shit on the north side of the bridge, de dum de dum de dum de dum!'

The Hull fans reciprocate on the south bank of the Humber.

Among the supporters of the home team is a large man in his forties with short blond hair and an earring. His finger gestures suggest he is looking for a fight, or maybe he even wishes to take on ten from south of the river. Finally, he shakes his hand, informing the Scunthorpe fans that they too masturbate. In this corner of the stadium there is so much glaring, so many gestures and insults that you lose focus on the game. Someone has smashed the ball against the crossbar.

Peter Taylor, who managed England for a short time, gets out of the Hull City dugout and scolds one of his players. The Scunthorpe end greets the former national coach.

'Peter Taylor is a wanker, is a wanker! Peter Taylor is a wanker, is a wanker!'

Hull's forwards combine well in front of the Iron defence, who stand rigid as the towers of the Humber Bridge. A Hull attacker lobs the ball over Evans and into the net. A nice goal. The Hull fans jeer:

'Who are you? Who are you?'

A man runs onto the pitch and two stewards escort him out.

Scunthorpe are playing terribly. Torpey has got himself a yellow card for getting embroiled with his marker. Taylor is the only one creating danger. When he gets the ball he attacks, gets into the box or goes down the flank looking to cross. He is exciting, ambitious.

A Hull striker gets the ball, knocks it out wide and runs into the six yard box where he meets the cross with a neat headed flick. Another good goal. They are asking again who we are. We are Brian Laws barmy army on the verge of a breakdown.

A teenage girl makes gestures to a man of about forty, telling him that he too is of course a wanker. The man is surrounded by other older supporters of Hull City. The girl, who is beautiful and is sitting with her boyfriend or brother, shows them two fingers, something the English find offensive.

A Hull city fan gestures towards someone in the away end, reproaching the size of his gut. Brian Laws leaves the bench to give instructions and someone shouts.

'This is shit, Laws!'

At the break, a man dressed as the mascot of Hull, in a tiger costume, invites the mascot of Scunthorpe, in a bunny costume, for a kick about. The Hull mascot seems friendlier. The rabbit is reluctant to play and, when he eventually kicks the ball, he does so with diffidence. The Tiger has football boots. 'Scunny Bunny' wears his big fancy dress shoes.

The PA announces a message from Vicky to Jason, who are both at the game: 'Will you marry me?' The public celebrate but, if Jason has gone to have a cup of tea, he might not have heard Vicky's proposal.

A local band, 59 Violets, play 'Dirty Water' in the centre circle. A mix between British psychedelia of the nineties and Americana of the Southern States.

Police in yellow jackets are patrolling the stadium, filming the segment where both sets of fans meet, with camcorders. This is the place in which almost all incidents occur.

Scunthorpe have sent twenty letters this year to people who buy tickets to sit specifically in the area closest to rival fans, explaining that their presence at Glanford Park is unwanted. Parents have to be able to take their children to a match without feeling the threat of violence, without exposing their kids to regular displays of brutality or verbal abuse.

The pub closest to the ground is now the source of all the problems due to the oppressive and effective security inside the stadium.

In the control room, the heads of security of both Scunthorpe and Hull are looking at screens showing images taken by cameras. Watching for a hint of trouble, or to see if any individual banned from football grounds has entered the stadium.

A succession of tragedies has changed the way in which people watch a football match. In the past, Scunthorpe fans sat or stood anywhere on an away trip, and the frequency of visits to clubs who played in the same division meant fans would be familiar and greet each other. That all changed in the seventies and eighties with hooliganism.

Alan Webster, head of security at Scunthorpe United, has a comprehensive guide in his office establishing the rules to be followed in all football grounds. It contains hundreds of pages regulating everything from the angle of the slope of the stands to the criteria for placement of containment fences still found in the fourth division. The guide explains procedures to prevent, contain and dissolve any pitch invasion. Webster also has the safety manual prepared by the Football Association, with instructions on what to do in case of a fire, or when a match is suspended after the gates have been opened but before kick-off, or if the PA system fails.

These procedures are performed by people specifically trained to obtain an official certificate as stewards for football matches. In 1982, the head of security had six under his command. Now he has to recruit sixty for big games.

The match against Yeovil Town was in the category NPI (No Police Inside). Only a few hundred fans made the long journey and, according to the security partner at Yeovil, didn't include any known hooligans. This one in Hull is a category C game, the highest risk category. It requires more than two hundred police officers together with stewards employed by the home club.

When Scunthorpe host a category C game, the club has to pay Humberside Police about £10,000. This pays for about twenty or thirty policemen. If the club had to face the full cost, it would come to about forty thousand pounds, all the gate money or more.

Alan Webster believes that a hooligan at a football match is also a hooligan in life. He is the guy who is giving people the eye in a pub spoiling for a fight. He never grows up. A yob in his youth unwilling to let go.

The second half gets under way. The fans respond.

'Iron, Iron, Iron.'

From the Hull end, a voice screams out at the away fans.

'Shut up.'

People laugh and then the away fans replicate.

'Hull is full of fuckers, it's a town full of fuckers.'

The game drifts into dullness until Scunthorpe score. People are now more interested.

A young man stands up, opens his arms out and shouts: 'Ooooohhhh, aaaahhhhhhh'. The response from the Hull crowd is sharp: 'Aaaaaaahhhhh, oooooooohhhhh'.

Has anybody noticed in the midst of this constant distraction that the Hull keeper seems incapable of dealing with high balls or the disappearance of Cleveland Taylor in the second half?

The PA announces the attendance as 19,076 spectators. Scunthorpe supporters talk about their rivals. Hull should not be playing in the fourth division. It is a large crowd but the home fans seem subdued in comparison to the away support.

The game ends. The defeated soldiers of Brian Laws barmy army go to the away end to applaud their fans, which correspond despite such a poor display against their rivals.

Visitors must squeeze through a narrow passage when leaving the ground, taking the occasional premeditated push by a Hull fan. Policemen with dogs patrol their short walk. They find a Hull fan marauding among the parked buses. He gestures innocence to the police before showing his two fingers and the masturbating swing to the Scunthorpe brethren.

A boy of about twelve, accompanied by adults, spits at the window of one of the buses in the convoy. The police block roads, and later the dual carriageway, to allow the defeated a safe return home.

Alan Webster, the head of security at Glanford Park, believes that days like today are symptoms of the deterioration of society. People did not lock the backdoor before going out. Now his mother does not dare to go outside at all. There is a lack of discipline in school and in life in general. Football hooliganism has no solution, according to him, until we return to a society based on mutual trust, on working together in a life which we share. He believes that one day we will get there and he defines this journey as some form of return.

A mediocre season to confirm continuity. Alex Calvo Garcia will say goodbye to Scunthorpe in the sullen spring of 2004. The hope of promotion dissipates during a long winter of injuries. This year could only be remembered for good fortunes in the Cup, culminating in an afternoon in January on the south coast

It has been thirty years since Scunthorpe reached the fourth round of the FA Cup. The draw brings silver to the clubs coffers with an away trip to Premier League Portsmouth. Sharing the gate receipts from Fratton Park and some television money will pay off debts and a couple of signings for next season. But the thousand or so who have made the trip to the naval city will not be satisfied with promises for next season.

After travelling for six hours by bus, Scunthorpe fans have to join a long queue to enter the ground. The only set of turnstiles for the away end is situated right next to two prefab toilets and a food van that sells burgers and chips. People buying food and going to the urinals block the entry.

The visitors terrace is the only part of the ground not covered. Cheap plastic seats are nailed into the concrete. An advertising hoarding on the stand opposite says: 'We can make your dreams a reality.'

A team of children from 'Pompey' do a lap of honour. An old man in a sailors cap, carrying some kind of banner, now wanders around giving the fans a military salute.

The day started bright but cold. When kick off approaches there is a dense black cloud hanging over the ground. Flood lights are switched on.

Football is a game which commences at three o'clock in the afternoon on an English Saturday.

'Brian Laws' barmy army! Brian Laws' barmy army!'

An insistent chorus makes a wave of noise, pushing Scunthorpe, holding 'Pompey' for thirty minutes. They run and fight. Peter Beagrie hits the side netting.

But at the other end there is more quality and danger. Israeli midfielder Eyal Berkovic is playing for the first time in front of his new club's fans and is busy. Short, lively, imaginative and with a nice touch, a veteran of the upper tiers of football. He tries to combine with the elegant Teddy Sheringham, who is in the penultimate stage of a career that saw him established in the England team.

The game is effectively over after half an hour. 'Pompey' score. A man with two or three teeth missing stands up and encourages everyone to join him.

'S and a C and a U, N, T. H and an O and an R, P, E. U, N, I and a T, E, D. Scunthorpe United F.C.'

Nobody responds. The best is gone. They have internationals in their ranks and good defenders.

But Matt Sparrow is in the box! Nothing comes of it and he falls to the ground injured. The fans are revived:

'Scunthorpe till I die! Scunthorpe till I die!'

There is a hint of renewed hope in the second half. The team presses high but attacks fade in over ambitious passes or a clumsy fall. Neat one-two between Harper and Berkovic, Sheringham blocks a defender and Matt Taylor gets the ball in the box. He drills his second of the game low and hard.

The home fans laugh from a distance.

'You're not singing anymore, you're not singing anymore!'

The afternoon has become cold and grey until a loose ball in the penalty area reaches Andy Parton who scores. A few minutes of childish hope: 'Come On!' Cheers with an aroma of desperation, long high balls, overzealous fouls, Laws agitated on the touchline.

The PA offers sweet goodbyes.

'Portsmouth Football Club would like to thank the supporters of Scunthorpe United Football Club and wish you a safe journey home.'

Farewell to the Cup. Thanks for the cash.

It is a slow walk to the train station; police with fluorescent jackets guide the fans, tangled passengers wait on a cold platform, a courteous melee to get to the carriage doors. Two elderly couples sit in front of each other. The Portsmouth fans explain to their northern companions that the club's new owner wants to rotate the stadium ninety degrees, but the council will not authorise the building of the new ground. The club's future is riding on it. Before they leave the train at their station, the Scunthorpe man tells them: 'We are happy enough.'

Great events are accompanied by marvels and omens, and the revolution in European football coincided with a strike of public sector employees in the Grand Duchy of Luxembourg. It was 15 December, 1995.

On that day, the European Court of Justice issued its judgement on the claim filed by Jean Marc Bosman against a Belgian club, RFC Liège, and against the European Union of Football Associations.

Bosman wanted to sign for French club DSL Dunkerque. But Liège refused the transfer and lowered his salary. Bosman filed a lawsuit in which his lawyers argued that the retention by football clubs of players whose contract had expired violated, among others, Article 48 of the Treaty of Rome, the foundation charter of the European Economic Community. It states that, 'free movement of workers entails the right to accept offers of employment actually made and to move freely for this purpose in the territory of the Member States.'

The court ruling in favour of Bosman broke the unique regulations in football, which had turned its professionals into a special case among European citizens and tied them to the interests and passions of supporters and directors.

The Professional Footballers Association had achieved the lifting of the maximum wage and freedom of contract but the Bosman ruling changed overnight the market for European Union footballers.

A few weeks before, Wigan Athletic had already opened the doors of the lower divisions of the English Football League to foreign players.

Dave Whelan, who played for Blackburn Rovers in the old First Division but had to quit the game after a serious injury, became a successful businessman. He had developed a grocery store into a chain of shops selling sports clothing and equipment.

His love of football led him to sponsoring the Wigan shirt, in which he had played as a youngster. He later bought the club and, after a business trip to Spain in the summer of 1995, he announced the fairly improbable signing of three foreign players for his Fourth Division club.

On arrival to the club, Roberto Martínez and Isidro Díaz from Balaguer, and Jesús Seba from Real Zaragoza were christened 'The Three Amigos' after the Mexican sombrero wearing gringos in the John Landis film.

In the summer of 1996, Hull City, also in the Fourth Division, signed Antonio Doncel, who had played the previous season at Racing Ferrol.

Meanwhile, back in Ordizia, Alex Calvo García has neither a team nor a job. And he speaks with his colleague in Beasain, Iñaki Ibáñez.

Ibáñez had played in front of a packed Santiago Bernabéu, on the beach with the Real Sociedad youth team, in Ondarroa and in Vitoria. At 21, he signed for Espanyol of Barcelona, in the Primera División of the Liga.

A few things were missing for Ibáñez to become a first class player. He had a good brain but the body did not respond to what his mind was thinking. He lacked the speed and the power required at the highest level. He continued his itinerary: Rayo Vallecano, Sestao, Eibar,...

When he returned to his home town of San Sebastián, he sold fuel and oil additives. He would occasionally visit Miguel Santos at his office to offer his help, if only answering the telephone.

Santos worked in a bank where employees left work in the early afternoon. He acted as intermediary in some signings for the local basketball team. In the summer of 1981, goalkeeper Vicente Biurrun asked him for help when he wanted to move from Real Sociedad to Osasuna. Santos became a football agent.

Latin American economies were bankrupt and the Berlin Wall had fallen. Footballers from the south and the east sought their fortune in the rich European market, where their asking price was also attractive to the clubs. After the Bosman ruling, the agent became an indispensable part of a more lucrative market.

Miguel Santos called Iñaki Ibáñez one day in 1988, at half past eight in the evening, to ask him if he could come to his office at once to give him a hand on a particularly busy day.

In the summer of 1996, Calvo García visits his friend Ibáñez, now established as a football agent working with Santos. It was he who recommended Jandro to Eibar. But two years later he is looking for work.

Jandro has spoken to his girlfriend Leire. They would not mind going abroad. England would be their preferred destination. They could learn a language which would help them later in their professional lives.

Ibáñez was keen to expand the agency business into the English market. He had some contacts with Italian agents through John Toshack. It was mentioned that a club called Scunthorpe was in the market for a striker.

Ibáñez sent Luis Garmedia, who had also been at Beasain. He played in a reserve league game at Chesterfield. Coach Mick Buxton told reporters: 'The boy didn't do too bad. He is going home this weekend and we will let him know. It is always difficult for someone to come to a foreign country to play, but Luis has a smattering of English to communicate.'

Three days later, Buxton announced his verdict to the local newspaper, the *Scunthorpe Telegraph*, 'We had to make a decision and for what I have seen of Luis he didn't offer us something better than what we have. He won't be coming back, but we are trying to bring another Spanish footballer next week. He is a centre-forward who was recommended to us and if all works well we can put him in the squad for Scarborough on Wednesday.'

On the following Saturday, the team lose one nil. The headline of the match report asks, 'Where will the goals come from?' Strikers John Eyre and Andy McFarlane scored 35 goals between them in the previous campaign but have just two so far this season.

Scunthorpe is looking for a goal scoring centre-forward and Jandro flies to Manchester. An employee of the agency contracted by Ibáñez is waiting for him. Jandro cannot speak a word of English and his driver not a word of Spanish. The two-hour drive to Scunthorpe is a long one. When he reaches Glanford Park, he is taken on another journey by minibus. The *Telegraph* detects an irony. 'From Spain to Scarborough!'

Alex Calvo García's first destination on English soil is a tourism town of healing waters, chilly beaches and donkey rides shaken by the growth of charter holidays to the Costa del Sol.

The local paper is on the trail. 'Scunthorpe United may play another Spanish player in the game tonight. He is Jandro, a centre-forward who is beginning a trial for a week.'

United are keen to sign a foreign player to emulate their rivals, Hull City, but Jandro was not the first immigrant to join the club. In 1957, John Gyorgy Jozsef Jellinek trained with the team. He had been a youth international in Hungary. He played with Puskas, Bozsik, Kocsis and Czibor, who were part of the national team whose victory at Wembley in 1953 astonished the inventors of the game. He had been coached by Janos Bogar, 'The Colonel', who watched his troops from the stand dressed in military uniform. Jellinek recalls in his autobiography, 'From Nowhere to Nowhere the Hard Way', his journey as a migrant, his success in business and his subsequent bankruptcy. He gave up football while in Scunthorpe, convinced that the British did not understand him.

The manager at that time was no less exotic. Frank Wong Soo, son of a Chinese father and an English mother, was the first ethnic minority footballer to represent England. He does not appear on the records since the FA does not recognise war time internationals. Soo spent three decades managing teams in Scandinavian countries before spending a year in charge of Scunthorpe. He was later manager of the Israeli national team.

In his first tortuous conversations with the help of hands and facial expressions, Jandro realises that nobody is going to pronounce his name right, so he suggests Alex as an alternative. He plays 45 minutes against Scarborough on a poor pitch, without spectators. He thinks that this is the stadium of Scarborough F.C. and wonders if this is what the famed football of the English looks like in the real world.

Alex plays as a centre-forward, a position he has never played before as a professional footballer. The team wins 3-0, their first points in the reserves league.

Vice Chairman Rex Garton knows that Buxton is a man of few words so he is not overly pessimistic when the manager gives his first impression: 'the lad's got something'. Garton and the chairman Keith Wagstaff are pleased. They want to sign the Spaniard, it is exotic, it would be good publicity, he would bring intrigue and excitement. If the guarded Buxton says the boy has something then the directors are thinking that he must be a phenomenon.

Buxton confirms as much in his post-match interview with the *Telegraph*. 'I am never one to get carried away with things and it is difficult to assess a player over such a short period, especially when there are also others on trial in the team, but I would say that my first impression of Jandro were favourable.'

It is late and dark when the team returns to Scunthorpe. Youth team coach Paul Wilson gives Alex a lift to his lodgings. He could tell Calvo García about the fragile ambitions of the professional footballer. Wilson had started with another Scunthorpe player, Russ Wilcox, at Frickley Athletic, where both were part of the England Non-League team. He was a useful striker in his years at Yeovil, top goalscorer in two seasons, but injuries and the opportunism of directors prevented him from signing for Football League clubs. Wilson could educate the Spaniard on the challenges that he would face but for the moment he has got lost trying to find his mute passenger's lodgings in a town that he still does not know well.

Finally, they find the home of John and Viola Rowbottom. After serving with the Royal Air Force, John is employed at the steelworks. Viola is from the Philippines and works as a nurse. She knows a few words of the old Spanish left in the islands by sailor-priests like Urdaneta. They have no children, and the club regularly sends them players who are on trial. Luis Garmendia had been there and made a good impression on his hosts. He spoke English and they would have liked him to stay.

Their new guest looks overwhelmed by the trip and the stress of a new environment in which he understands almost nothing.

John tries to reassure Alex.

'Don't worry, *señor*'

Alex does not respond.

'*Hablo tu Ingles?*' asks Viola.

'No', replies Alex.

'Oh, dear, we have a problem', muses John.

Alex is tired and goes to his bedroom.

In the following days, he attends training. He understands practically nothing of what his new team-mates are saying. He is Manuel from Barcelona. Every evening, on returning to John and Viola's home, Alex repeats the same sentence.

'I tired, go bed.'

He devours bananas and maintains silence but the landlords like their lodger. He is courteous and eats whatever Viola cooks.

Alex takes stock of each day: he has not talked to anyone.

He telephones his girlfriend and then listens to 'Sweet dreams', a song by 'El Último de la Fila' (Last in the Queue) on his Walkman: 'Sad eyes looking at maps, nowhere to go, nowhere to go back... Take my hand and sleep by my side; if you don't mind...'

John finally finds a way of communicating. He plays blackjack with Alex on the kitchen table.

Scunthorpe is not a happy club. The *Telegraph* publishes an angry letter from a fan. He provides his name, his fifteen years old membership number and the exact location of his seat. The Iron are eighteenth in the table. And the next match is against their big rivals, Hull City.

It is not the manager's fault. The directors are to blame. And the fan makes three suggestions to them. 'Firstly: That they get their hands in their pockets and offer finances for new players. Secondly: Selling the club to someone or a consortium which are willing to commit to the first suggestion. Thirdly: They shut the club down due to lack of interest.'

'The fans (a dwindling band) of the club are fed up of being promised better results next season,' writes the correspondent, and he finishes the article with a poignant postscript, 'Did the chairman's wife return the £270 to the club that she won at the 50/50 draw?'

Alex, the mute, travels that day on the team bus to a place called Hereford. In the dressing room he begins to undress. His team-mates gesture to him that it is not necessary, he is not playing. The travels of Manuel from Ordizia make people laugh.

He starts in a match for the first time on a Wednesday night at Glanford Park. He now understands that there are two leagues, one for the first team and one for the reserves; his league. Darlington are the visitors. Few people are watching. He plays ninety minutes.

'It was a competitive game against quality opposition and I think the boy did well,' Buxton tells reporters, who ask whether the club will be signing the foreigner. 'I have to sit down with

Alexander before deciding anything.'

On the following Friday, on the eve of the first match against Hull for twelve seasons, the club secretary, Don Rowing, takes Alex to the boardroom after he has finished his lunch in the club canteen.

It is a room with a large table, chairs and claret and blue curtains. In a small glass cabinet, the trophies won by the club. The most beautiful is a silver plate with the inscription, 'The Match, 1979'. This encounter, deserving of such a beautiful commemoration, was against Stevenage yet nobody seems to remember what was at stake.

The *Telegraph* hits the streets that afternoon with its back page carrying a headline playing with the memory of summer holidays and the present economic plight of the club: 'Alex no 'Costa' much.'

He is handed a contract until the end of the season. The club offer him 525 pounds a week, which is double of what he was earning at Eibar. The chairman has asked his daughter Nicola, who works in a travel agents and speaks Spanish, to help as interpreter. 'If you fall in pitch, the boss says you stay in pitch one moment more than necessary'. A slightly confusing football Spanish.

Buxton asks Alex whether he has suffered any serious injuries during his career. Nicola, the improvised translator, makes the comic mistake of the day. She asks Alex if he has ever suffered any serious slander during his career. Injuries is 'lesiones' in Spanish and slander is 'injurias'. Alex is now convinced that the English are indeed a strange breed.

Later that afternoon, he is posing in his new shirt, sponsored by the Cleethorpes theme park, 'Pleasure Island'.

That same weekend, Arsenal unveils Frenchman Arsène Wenger as the first foreign manager of a First Division club since the brief tenure of Slovakian Dr. Josef Venglos at Aston Villa.

John and Viola are delighted for Alex. He calls home. Is Leire going to pack her bags? And then they celebrate. Viola cooks a feast of potato omelettes. John gets the cards out. The boy from Ordizia pronounces some solemn words before the cards are dealt. 'I contract, beer'.

The next day, 5 October, 1996, Alex crosses the estuary of the Humber in the team bus. Their rivals, Hull City, await them in their old stadium, Boothferry Park. Alex gets changed. This time nobody stops him. He takes to the field to warm up and realises that he has finally landed in English football. It was not the playing field in Scarborough, nor an empty Glandford Park from three days ago. It was the shouting and these chants, the English passion for sport on a day of gala and fury.

Hull are unbeaten in ten and Scunthorpe have not won all month. When Mick Buxton reads out the first eleven – Samways, Hope, Wilson, Sertori, Walsh, Bradley, Housham, Gavin, Baker, D'Auria, Clarkson – Alex knows that he is on the bench. It is understandable. The manager has trouble communicating with the man brought in to match the exoticism of Hull's very own Antonio Doncel. Alex feels awkward when Buxton is instructing him. He feels embarrassed when he taps his foot and says to him: 'Foot, foot'. 'Alex from Ordizia' finally understands. Buxton is saying that football is a game played with your feet.

After thirteen minutes, Gavin is injured. Buxton tells Alex to get ready. It is a sudden immersion into a mutual battle of erosion. In every tackle and every run, in every disputed ball, everybody seems to be playing for their lives. His lungs are going to explode. Alex dribbles past his marker and receives a hard kick. He is continuously blocked with an elbow to his face and finally suffers a cut lip. He throws a punch to his opponent in response. It is a nervous reaction after days of anxiety and now he is terrified. To come on as a substitute and return to the stand as a weak foreigner, a bleeding child from the southern climates unable to take the first inevitable hit in a fight against real men from the English north. Or even worse, being sent off in the eternal colours of the club that has just given him a contract, leaving the impression that they had signed one of those temperamental types, with a brain overheated by the sun.

Nothing happens. He runs and fights, but he fails to score the goal which he was signed for. Having missed pre-season training, Buxton sees that the tempo of the game is taking its toll on the recently landed Spaniard. He is substituted in the eighty-sixth minute. Fans applaud him. Scunthorpe score twice. The second is from lower leagues journeyman striker Paul Baker, signed by Buxton to score goals, the presumed task of Scunthorpe's first foreign signing.

In the dressing room, a team-mate tells Alex that someone wants to speak to him outside. A tall man with greying hair greets Alex in Spanish. He tells him that his name is John Costello and he introduces his wife Val. They are both Scunthorpe fans.

John tells Alex that he knows how it feels when you want to say something but you are unable to. He gives him his telephone number. John is a retired French and Spanish teacher and he is willing to give Alex free English lessons in his house.

Viola, Alex's landlady, also helps him to sort out his new life. On Monday, she takes him out shopping for clothes. While he is trying on some trousers, the shop assistant remarks: 'Lucky you!' When they go to open a bank account Viola asks if anyone can help him. The young woman replies: 'I'd do whatever he wants. Is he single?'

When he goes to set up his social security number, the ladies in the office come to have a closer look at the new Latin idol in this pale region of North Lincolnshire. The manager of the office quips: 'I've never seen anything like it. I didn't know Scunthorpe had so many female fans'.

The *Telegraph* is to blame. It has published several photos of the new footballer in town. On that same Monday the paper shows the foreigner doing an overhead kick. Alex has dark hair, green eyes. He has the looks of a movie star. Rex Garton, the vice chairman of the club, knows that the board has scored a public relations goal. Football has delivered something truly exotic to the town García.'

He visits John and Val, and the teacher educates Alex on football and English life: 'This is a small town and the club doesn't have a lot of money, but we support it with all our heart and that's what matters.'

Costello comes from an Irish-Scottish family but he was born in Scunthorpe. His father worked in the steelworks and had seven children, all of whom attended University; John to King's College in London. When he was twenty-one he travelled to Bilbao to work in the University of Deusto as an assistant in the English language department.

Since returning to Scunthorpe in 1974 to teach, he has followed the team home and away. His brother played with Kevin Keegan in the youth team and he will always support the local side, even in the Fourth Division: 'The true fan follows the club because it is a team, a form of solidarity, of identity. No matter where they are in the table or which division. Football was regional and the club represented the town. All that has changed since the eighties. It has happened in society on the whole. People love celebrities. They travel long distances to watch Liverpool or Manchester United. They want to be moved by success.'

Society and football, explains John Costello, have become more materialistic: 'We are influenced by the American culture of winners. If you do not win, people become negative. You have to sack the manager if he loses two games. It is a shame. I like the idea of the team. And people can be unrealistic. We will never be in the Premier League. Where would we get the money? People are only interested in glory, victory. But I think that some local identity is important, some pride in your town. And following Scunthorpe you can see a good football match.' Alex listens to Costello's words, which resonate with the spirit that drove Real Sociedad.

The generous host informs Alex that North Lincolnshire is a land populated by descendants of Vikings, a warrior tribe. 'That affects the style of play. If you tackle hard you are a good player. The fans appreciate cold aggression and grit and do not like their players rolling over three times or protesting to the referee. The traditional attitude is stoic. During World War II, parliament debated the treatment of German prisoners in Britain, while Hitler was bombing the country. We are proud that things are done according to the rules. When the English played amongst themselves these traditions remained strong and intact. When we started to compete with others everything gradually changed. Our players learned good and bad things. The best players in the Premiership do not drink as much as they drank but they dive. If we are cheating, I get no satisfaction in winning'.

Alex is a diligent student. He is learning English and about the history of football and of the country in which it was invented.

Games to keep possession of an object or to place it somewhere are an ancient and widespread pastime. They are still played in Sedgefield or Lincoln, where men from different quarters of a village recreate these rowdy games with fuzzy rules. Such games were also played in public schools where the elite sent their sons. Walls, mounds, trees or marks on the ground defined the rules.

Most of those schools changed in the second half of the nineteenth century. Parents wanted better learning in the society of the industrial revolution and of empire. They did not want their sons to be taught by single men, whose often crude religious faith was their only qualification and who seemed to enjoy living among boys in an atmosphere of relative brutality. The schools opened their doors to married teachers, embracing the athletic Christianity championed in the writings of Thomas Hughes and others.

Hughes wrote, *Tom Brown's School Days*, to give faith to English boarding schools. The author of the novel, published in 1857, argues in the preface to the sixth edition the benefits of an alliance with Prussia, 'the most natural and healthy for Protestant England'. The first chapter of the book depicts an idyllic life in Berkshire, home to the family of the protagonist, Thomas Brown.

At parish fairs, families cook cakes and youths compete in duels of back-sword, whose aim is to 'smash the head' of the rival with a stick. Hughes writes in his autobiographical novel, trying to inspire the sentimental education of young Englishmen, that equality and inequality never entered the minds of the Brown brothers but when they were running, fighting or climbing.

Tom Brown leaves Berkshire when he is eleven. Riding overnight in an open carriage on the journey between home and the school of Rugby, he notes shortly after the beginning of his trip that he has never known a November night so cold. He cannot feel his legs but he is taken by something deeper, 'the consciousness of silent endurance, so dear to every Englishman, of standing out against something, and not giving in.'

He arrives in the morning at the school that will create, under the direction of Thomas Arnold, the model for the reform of private schools in England. The headmaster is a man who left his local vicarage due to his shyness and had achieved national relevance advocating Catholic emancipation. He acquired a great reputation for transforming school governance by the eulogies of former pupils, like Hughes. More cautious historians attribute him two main reforms.

To contain the frequent rebellions and the prevalence of bullying, Arnold introduced the prefects system, which structured the student community by seniority. The older boys were made responsible for maintaining discipline in their residence. Novices, or fags, became their charges in the first steps of their school life. The second reform was to fuse teaching and morality. The curriculum, with classical languages and history as the main pillars, was not altered, but his sermons at Sunday Mass were to become an essential part of learning. For Arnold, first came religious and moral principles, then gentlemanly conduct and intellectual ability. He provided character to those educated to execute power in the complex and disorderly world of industry and empire.

Sports, and in particular organised team sports, were an ideal instrument to instil in youngsters the required personal qualities, according to Hughes. In the ten years that followed the publication of his book, the first Open Championship of golf and the first athletic championship were held, the first England cricket team left for Australia and the Football Association was founded. Tom Brown's adventures were as well a major intellectual influence on Pierre de Coubertin, founder at the end of the nineteenth century of the modern Olympic movement.

Mihir Bose, author of *The Spirit of the Game*, searched at the beginning of the twenty-first century for references to sport in all known writings and printed preachings of Thomas Arnold without finding a single mention. Arnold's pleasures were bathing and walking. But the canonical version of the headmaster's love of competitive sports had been established by the embellishments of Thomas Hughes and the international diplomacy of the French baron at a time of great social transformations.

Tom Brown discovers 'football' on his first day at school, which pits the residents in two student houses. It is a messy game, a primitive rugby in which unequal numbers of contenders are vying for possession of a ball, with long kicks, scrums, tackles and runs in order to score by placing the ball behind the goal line. All told by Hughes in a chronicle of outstanding heroes and hopeless cowards. The new pupil wins his first decorations, as God may have intended, in the last minute: leaving the watching crowd he rushes into battle for the ball without regard to his puny body.

He is wounded and triumphant but remains a 'fag' who has to endure the abuse of the bully Flashman. Only by stoically accepting a tumbling in a bed sheet by older students does he earns immunity.

He spends his time hunting hares or bird watching. When one day he is caught breaking the rules, he accepts the reasoning of the headmaster to be punished with the cane. Spending the first year of school life in rough camaraderie was the staple education for the sons of rich families.

But one day, in the new term, a physically weak and delicate novice, Arthur, is harassed. On his first infernal night in Rugby, he bends his knee before bed to pray. Tom Brown, who had lied to his mother about his forgetfulness of daily rites, becomes a man through compassion. Brown also kneels in prayer, completing the portrait of the hero of the novel, the good Christian who prays, studies and fights: 'Once to every man and nation comes the moment to decide/ In the strife of Truth with Falsehood, for the good or evil side ... Then it is the brave man chooses, while the coward stands aside, Doubting in his abject spirit, till his Lord is crucified.'

Thomas Hughes quotes the verses of his contemporary, James Russell Lowell, poet, writer against slavery and United States Ambassador to Spain.

A Christian with muscle is the ideal of man. When Brown accepts the challenge of Slogger Williams to a fight, for standing in the way of a beating of Arthur, who has embarrassed the bullies with his sentimentality and application, the novelist becomes poetic about war: 'What would life be without fighting, I should like to know? From the cradle to the grave, fighting, rightly understood, is the business, the real highest, most honest business of every son of man. Every one who is worth his salt has his enemies, who must be beaten, be they evil thoughts and habits in himself, or spiritual wickedness in high places, or Russians, or Border-ruffians, or Bill, Tom, or Harry, who will not let him live his life in quiet till he has thrashed them'. Hughes criticises the pacifist creed of Quakers, because for them 'human nature is too strong.' 'The world might be a better world without fighting, for anything I know, but it wouldn't be our world', he writes, 'and therefore I am dead against crying peace when there is no peace, and isn't meant to be.' There were wars in Crimea and in India when Hughes published his book, one of those Victorian novels heavy as an imperial crown.

Fortunately, everything ends in a game of cricket; much more than a game, it is 'the birthright of British boys old and young, as habeas corpus and trial by jury are of British men', says know-it-all Arthur. 'The discipline and reliance on one another which it teaches is so valuable,' concurs master Arnold, 'I think it ought to be such an unselfish game. It merges the individual in the eleven; he doesn't play that he may win, but that his side may.'

The protagonist, Tom Brown, declares the verdict: 'That's very true, and that's why football and cricket, now one comes to think of it, are such much better games than fives or hare-and-hounds, or any others where the object is to come in first or to win for oneself, and not that one's side may win.'

The best from Rugby were playing in front of them against a team of gentlemen donning the colours of Marylebone Cricket Club.

Pupils of Harrow, Eton, Shrewsbury, Charterhouse, Westminster or Rugby later progressed to university, where they wanted to play football in winter.

It was in Cambridge, in 1848, where the first common rules were agreed. Experimental games served to quash some dilemmas. Could the ball be passed forward or only backwards? What role the feet have in all this? Is the game to be played with fifty or twenty on each team? Should hacking be banned? What would be the consequences of heading the ball, which had different shape, weight and skin depending on the geography of schools or how air could be introduced into a pig's dried bladder? Groups of alumni formed the first clubs and others followed.

In the sixteenth and seventeenth century disputes over religion were what we now understand as politics. Henry VIII had proclaimed his sovereignty in opposition to the Roman pope, but his church felt uncomfortable with the spread of more stringent versions of Protestantism. The kingdom was divided between supporters of the established Church and dissenters- Quakers, Baptists, Methodists, Presbyterians... - who followed the Gospels as the only truthful instructions of how to live and govern on earth.

They were persecuted. Alternative dissenter academies emerged for the training of priests and laymen. The theory of predestination and its consequences were the subject of the schism.

In the seventeenth and eighteenth centuries dissenters' academies introduced a curriculum based on the learning of English, Mathematics and Science. They were essential tools for the interpretation of the will of God by people burdened with the knowledge that a supreme being already knew if they would face salvation or condemnation.

Personalities grown and educated among dissenters were behind many of the scientific and technical innovations that, along with private appropriation of common land, were at the origin of the industrial revolution defining the modern world.

Some of the first football clubs were set up by Methodist chapels, whose members also understood the benefits of muscular Christianity for the education of children. Other clubs were founded by men of industry and commerce in the new sprawling cities. They were familiar with rules and competition.

SCUNTHORPE HASTA LA MUERTE

In the first half of the nineteenth century, Parliament reduced the working hours for women and children. The emerging trade unions were able to gradually extend this to men. The industrial working class had Saturday afternoons free from work or religious duties, something unknown in the agrarian society. And many dedicated this time of leisure to games.

The new clubs formed the first associations. In 1863, after heated discussions in the Freemason's Tavern in London, they became the forefathers of 'soccer' or association football. During their discussions on whether players would be allowed to run with the ball after catching it in the air, or should wait for the first bounce, or whether hacking on the front side of the leg should be permitted, some clubs formed a Rugby Football Union and went their own way.

According to Dave Russell, author of *Football and the English*, soccer offered social benefits, colour, spectacle, emotions and more. Local rivalries were stoked when they organised the first cups, while the rugby clubs rejected competitions beyond a single game.

Simplicity imposed itself, football had 14 rules and rugby 59. And equality brought its premium. Even though the game was rougher than it is now – you could, for example, charge the goalkeeper when he had the ball – association football was a game for men of all sizes and more popular among those who had to earn their living working during the week, not able to afford serious injury to their bodies.

About a quarter of the first football clubs were associated with churches or chapels. The most victorious in those early days was Aston Villa, formed by the parishioners of a Methodist chapel in Lozells, a suburb of Birmingham. Others, like Everton, were established in pubs, operating at the time as social and transport hubs and keen to retain customers and attract new ones. Clubs were formed in factories. In Woolwich Arsenal, the 'Gunners'. West Ham was initially known as the Thames Ironworks.

Clubs wishing to win trophies in the industrial regions of Lancashire or the Midlands charged spectators and paid their best players cash in hand or by some form of indirect compensation. The governing elites of the first associations proclaimed these practices as unworthy, a perversion of sport. The game was just a game and the emergence of professionalism would pervert the fundamentals of its creation, it would make it just another business.

Once again, a recurring battle in the late nineteenth century was fought amongst aspiring traders and those with claims to nobility. The traders, which included many northerners, saw no hindrance in competitions between clubs with different budgets or in importing Scottish 'maestros' of the new game. Their world, industry and the market, responded to the ideal of salvation through rigour and effort. Their life was a constant competition. More graceful men did not want to debase themselves playing for victory but to enjoy athletic effort and display skills and good manners.

'A respectable man is degraded by playing with professionals,' said W. H. Jope, director of the Football Association of Birmingham, in one of the meetings held to resolve the social dilemma of the game. He defended the gratuitousness of physical exertion and the noble handshake at the end of battle.

Dave Russell quotes the prophecy by the *Manchester Guardian* of an irredeemable social split with the introduction of professionals. The idea had been to unite all classes 'in perfect equality', but rugby will become an aristocratic pastime and soccer would march towards extinction in southern England.

Letters were published complaining that the equilibrium sought by the rules will be mocked by those who hold an advantage of working in jobs that require physical effort. Others noted with sadness that the steps taken would lead to the dominance of the richest clubs. The introduction of betting creates alarm and so too the excitement of partisan crowds. Professional football is expanding as the century reaches its end, turning what should have been a haven of pleasure and virtue into just another job. Warnings are voiced that professional footballers have much of the day free and are a bad example for the youth of the working classes.

In January, 1884, Upton Park from London complain because Preston played against them with a team made up entirely of professionals. The Football Association expels the Lancastrians causing 31 clubs to leave in protest. The FA reconvene and avoids the split by ruling that affiliated clubs can pay a player who is born or has lived for at least two years within a six mile radius of its ground.

Professionals must be registered. They lined up in blue, like the overalls in the factory, to differentiate them from amateurs playing in limpid white. When England introduced a team of professionals in a match against Scotland, *The Athletic News* speculated that paid players would have been more congenial with the only amateur in the team, who was the captain, if he had not decided to ignore them on the long train journey, traveling in another compartment and behaving like a superior human being.

The newspaper also offered the recipe to prevent the game falling into the hands of a new class, skilled in the technique of football: 'It is possible to commit a player to a club for the whole season and submit these professionals to greater discipline than currently exists... In the new system it should be instilled into players that they are only servants of those who pay their wages. Therefore, those who have been hostile to employing professionals have the means, if they want to use them, to maintain strict discipline on this class being created. The Clubs that employ these professional players will be happy to have this strong authority over them.'

The transfer of Alf Common to Middlesbrough for one thousand pounds caused outrage. Amateur clubs of the south and professional clubs of the north formed different associations.

The directors had to lay down new rules. A competition should not be won by money alone. The game required uncertainty, which could not occur if the wealthy owners simply bought the best professionals; often coming from Scotland to earn their wages with their efficient style of team play, while the amateurs obtusely earned their defeat by engaging in narcissistic dribbling.

A free market would empower those who were already the strongest, it was argued. So a maximum wage of four pounds a week was imposed. Clubs also had the right to retain players against their will with a transfer system being put in place. English football at last had, if not quite what their Christian prophets had imagined, an improved competition. The sacrifice of those grand old ideals spurred great success.

At the end of their shift on Saturdays, the employees of the factories went to the ground to watch their team. The railway was spreading through Britain. In 1853, it carried a hundred million people and had a network of seven thousand miles, in 1883 there were 665 million passengers and twenty-five thousand miles of lines. Birmingham was less than four hours from Manchester and big games of the new League caused large movements of crowds.

The idea of a league, promoted by a director of Aston Villa, ignited across the country. Lower regional leagues were founded. Referees began to come under fire, mild insults were traded with rivals and there were even clashes between fans. And all because the working class had taken up a game created by elites and managed by the middle classes. The players and their followers were factory workers, children from textile mills grown up, which in the absence of anything else on Saturday had an appointment with the dummy and the pass, with the ballet of the proletariat, with the new tactics of the two-three-five and three-two-five; always five in attack in those brave times. Spectators with a longer memory complained that the new football was overly scientific. There were fewer goals but enthusiasm did not wane. In 1888 there were a thousand clubs. In 1905, ten thousand. The final of the FA Cup in 1888 was held in front of 17,000 spectators. In 1913, 121,919 went through the turnstiles. The early twentieth century was the golden age of football crowds. Goodison Park, Everton's stadium, held seventy thousand spectators. Manchester United built a new ground in Old Trafford, with a capacity for eighty thousand. And the British, who exploited mines in Huelva or built ships in Bilbao, spread their football around the world.

At the start of First World War, the English populace continued playing football and watching football games. The rugby scrum immediately disbanded to answer the call of king and country. Rudyard Kipling, poet of the empire, complained in *The Islanders* about his people, 'humbled by wisdom, mighty by sacrifice' whose souls seemed contented 'with the flannelled fools at the wicket or the muddied oafs at the goals.'

It also worried trade unionists, who, after reducing the working time of its people, now saw the danger of producing a race of workers who were only able to obey their masters and think about football, the stuff of which slaves are made, according to 'Gavroche', in an article published in 1904 in *Labour Leader*.

But the new heroes of the workers are wearing shorts and running after a ball, and the slaves become furious because some are City and others are United, United, United till we die.

Leire flies to Manchester. Scunthorpe United's alluring foreigner and his girlfriend are going to give it a go. They have nothing to lose.

Alex often finds himself on the bench and the club is not doing well. But Mick Buxton appreciates some qualities of his new signing:

'Alex is the type of player who will work instinctively,' he tells the press. 'Unlike others, he doesn't have to wait for me to tell him to work.'

A cultural revolution is shaking English football. Arsène Wenger, a polyglot from Alsace, stamps a new imprint on Arsenal.

The club with a reputation for tactical refinement under Herbert Chapman had become boring, boring Arsenal towards the end of the century. George Graham, a player of flair in his day, was an architect of tight defences as manager.

He had been fired on charges of receiving backhanders from transfer fees. Bruce Rioch took charge. He may have inherited the military spirit from his father, who had served in the armed forces, but his efforts to instil simplicity and discipline in the team did not work. Arsenal seems disoriented when the board brings in Wenger, after fulfilling his contract to the very end with Grampus Eight in Japan.

Wenger grew up in a Catholic family in Duttlenheim, a small community of 2,500 people, twenty kilometres from Strasbourg. His parents had a restaurant, 'La Croix d'Or', where supporters, directors, managers and players of the local team met regularly. He religiously attended matches and school, later taking a degree in economics. He was nothing special as a player but was an adept student of the game, travelling to various countries to watch matches and gather information about clubs, tactics and players.

He is met in English football with suspicion. The new coach expresses himself in an unusual way. He seems distant, analytical, cold. On his first day in charge of training the Arsenal players understand that everything has changed. There is no screaming. His planning is minute. He times each training exercise. Under his guidance, the club expands the budget for the medical department and build new facilities: heated pitches for winter, a residence for young trainees, a communal dining room. He forces a new diet to a team in which there are two avowed alcoholics. Fish and chips and fry-ups become the past. The times of pasta and lean meats have arrived.

A student of sports psychology, reader of business management manuals and biographies of exemplary lives, Wenger admires Arthur Rubinstein, who was still playing the piano with virtuosity into his eighties. He tells his players that the goal in life is to enjoy what one loves for as long as possible. If the veteran members of the squad follow his instructions they could prolong their careers and extend the extraordinary life of a football player.

A new philosophy of the game is instilled into the executioners of boring football. Endeavour is not only aimed to frustrate rivals but also to an aesthetic end. Passing, speed, movement, athletic harmony. Beauty as inspiration for the crowd.

Aspirations at Glanford Park are less glamorous. Mick Buxton is failing to improve the team with his own diet. He has hired Mark Lillis as his assistant. A former player at the club, he brings new training methods, but the atmosphere in the dressing room is strained. Veterans on the final days of their careers no longer accept orders from anyone. Buxton is fired in February. The board chooses Brian Laws as his substitute, the only player in the squad who has performed at the top level and with the necessary coaching badges.

Laws biography as a footballer reads well. Born in Wallsend, he would probably have wanted to play for his home-town team, Newcastle, but the promising striker with Wallsend Boys Club, which had produced a long list of professional players, was scouted by Burnley, where he signed as an apprentice at 16.

An injury in a clash of heads led his coach to move him to right back as a safety precaution. Homesick, tired by the chores of training and cleaning the stands, resentful of pros with requirements of starlets about the meticulous polishing of their boots, the young Laws finally made his home in Burnley as a number two.

He left after six years frustrated with a new manager who had a reputation for paying over the odds to sign friends with long careers in the lower divisions. After a brief spell with Huddersfield, coached by Mick Buxton, he returned to the north-east with Middlesbrough, who were heading towards financial trouble.

Laws was a key player at a club with no cash. In his second season, a new manager arrived. He was Bruce Rioch, a disciplinarian who asked his players 'to go like hell in tackles' during training. They were not paid regularly and on Laws' third season they found the gates of Ayresome Park padlocked. Being the skipper, he led a group of players, including Peter Beagrie, to a tribunal in which they were told that they were free to leave if the club failed to pay their salaries. Rioch went from house to house with a briefcase, handing out notes and cheques to the stadium stars of Saturday, struggling to pay for food, children's clothes and mortgages.

They won promotion but the new manager of Scunthorpe United could hardly celebrate. Laws had been carrying a cruciate ligament tear in his knee, which finally broke while taking a penalty against Bristol Rovers. Team success cannot allay the fear of ending your career at twenty-three.

After a year of rude rehabilitation, during which he started his training to be a coach, Laws rejoined a team winning promotion again, this time to the First Division. But in the summer Rioch only offered him a one-year contract and for less money than had previously been agreed. He felt cheated, and trapped in a club that could keep him on their books without a contract until some other club paid a transfer fee. Then Ronnie Fenton phoned.

Fenton was Brian Clough's assistant manager. Clough was already a member of the Pantheon of great English football managers alongside the likes of Herbert Chapman, Bill Shankly or Alf Ramsey.

Brian Laws had already worked in his brief career under managers who were flash, bad or utterly mad, and in his autobiography, *Laws of the Jungle*, he sets the scene of his welcome to Nottingham Forest by "the most famous face in football at the time".

'Welcome to the club. But I just want to ask you something. Are you a good player or a bad player?' asked Clough to his new recruit.

The glory years were just a memory in 1988 but Forest was still one of the best in the First Division, playing a game based on possession, speed and movement.

Laws was a good full back, with a physique to compete and a brain trained to do the simple things right. There were England internationals in that Forest team: Des Walker, Stuart Pearce, Teddy Sheringham and the coach's son, Nigel Clough. And they had Roy Keane, an Irish teenager who would become the Premier League's most influential player in the nineties when he moved to Manchester United.

The English game was ruled by brute percentages. How many long balls could fall to the feet of a team-mate after a rebound? Hard runners able to harass and tackle were leaving their stamp on a supposed national style, while successful teams like Liverpool saw ball retention as the first step to scoring a goal and preventing their rivals from doing so.

Brian Clough's teams were nice to watch and referees saw Clough as some kind of saint. He condemned foul play and fined his own players for complaining.

But disgusted with the German referee he refused to give a press conference to Italian journalists- 'cheating bastards'- after his Derby County were knocked out in the semi-finals of the European Cup by Juventus.

Brian Clough and his assistant, Peter Taylor, a sporting and theatrical double act, won the First Division title with Derby County and Nottingham Forest and two European Cups. Only Tom Watson and Herbert Chapman had won the English title with two different teams. Only Kenny Dalglish has done so since Clough, achieving it with two small provincial clubs. No club the size of Forest had won the European

Cup before 1978 and none after Clough, who had won it twice.

He would send flowers to the wives of his players and gave money to people in difficulty. The best coach of his time dreamed of leading England out at Wembley to redeem the country from the occupants of the FA seats, who feared or despised him. He is known in the culture of football as a hero who swears and drinks, destroying himself while aiming to raise the hopes of the damned for an end to corruption.

In 2005, the Nottingham Playhouse Theatre Company staged *The Spirit of the Man*, a play by Stephen Lowe, in which Old Big 'ead appears as an angelic ghost to a playwright, Jimmy, who is suffering writer's block.

Brian: 'You called, young man?'

Jimmy screams in shock

Brian: 'Sorry, son, didn't mean to make you jump out your skin. Have you clocked who I am? Speak up. Eh, you're not one of them foreigners they keep shipping in, are you? Bloody bonkers. Half the Premier League spend more time chatting the birds up at Berlitz than they do out on the pitch. Speakie the English?'

Jimmy, the dramatist, is not interested in football, but he saw the manager of Forest marching with the miners against the government of Margaret Thatcher in 1984 and believes that 'Thatcher beat the miners and made it rain all the time, all the time for a generation.'

His imagination has dried up and he is in an existential crisis, but the cast is waiting for characters and dialogue. Clough, in customary green jersey, guides him to his protagonist, Robin Hood, as a redeemer, a leader of the outlaws who inspires in them the dream of changing the world.

Brian: 'He (Robin Hood) gathered together a whole bunch of waifs and strays, flotsam and bloody jetsam, them that nobody wanted, like my Forest team in ´78 and...'

Jimmy: 'And what?'

Brian: 'What did he do? He turned them into the merriest bloody band in the land.'

Jimmy: 'So they weren't merry before?'

Brian: 'Course they weren't. They were absolutely bloody miserable, flea-infested, homeless, pox-ridden, playing for crap teams in the wrong position, sick to the rafters with a diet of nettle soup and roll-ups. And what made them merry?'

Jimmy: 'Was it the sacred mushroom? Or putting on funny hats and singing 'YMCA' under the greenwood tree?'

Brian: 'It was me... Robin Hood.'

'Robin Clough' can not heal the pessimism of Jimmy. It still rains incessantly over him and his protagonist, who finally confesses to having betrayed his band with the illusion of hope. 'Hide yourself, hide yourself, my friends. Hide your face from one another lest you leave the trace of desire and hope. Only the fool fights. Hide.'

Brian Laws, Scunthorpe's new boss, played under the latter day Clough, abandoned by Taylor, doubtful about his ability to reproduce the magic of the old times. Engrossed in a paternalistic pose, delighted in eccentricity and forever searching for a fast and delicate style of play. In 1990, he sat on the bench while his team were lying down on the grass waiting to start extra time in the FA Cup final at Wembley. He was already lost in a dense alcoholic cloud, which in 1993 forced him to abandon football in a pitiful physical state after taking Forest back to the Second Division to where he had begun.

In December 1994, Laws left Nottingham Forest to become player manager of Grimsby Town. He started well, making good signings in the transfer market and was offered a three-year contract. The 'Mariners' made the news when, after a collection among fans, they brought Italian striker Ivano Bonetti to the fishing town at the mouth of the Humber. Bonetti had won the Scudetto and the Intercontinental Cup with Juventus.

But in the second season everything unravelled. Bonetti was unfit, would take a relaxed view of training, defending and teamwork. He was prone to tantrums and insisted on being accompanied by an interpreter even in the dressing room. In February at Luton, the team lost 3-2 and a row escalated into a fight. Did Bonetti throw a chicken leg at Laws while being berated for a miserable performance? Perhaps. But what most people said, until Laws published his autobiography in 2012, was that the manager threw a plate with chicken legs towards Bonetti and broke a bone in his face. No, it wasn't like that. Brian Laws did the damage on the Italian's cheekbone with a left hook.

It was only football. Alex Ferguson, knighted by this point, cut David Beckham's eyebrow after kicking a boot in the Manchester United dressing room. When Lawrie McMenemy, then Southampton manager, rebuked defender Mark Wright, the two ended up locked in the shower. Cambridge coach John Beck and striker Steve Claridge had a fist fight. Brian Clough hit several players during his tenure at Forest. Laws had already floored a team-mate at Forest, Des Walker.

Bonetti filed a lawsuit against Laws. The damage to his reputation for that incident and some bad results on the pitch got him sacked by Grimsby.

He found himself at Darlington and, in January 1997, Mick Buxton signed him for Scunthorpe. Times were hard. The team was on a run of home defeats. The seventh sparked protests from supporters.

Fans wrote to the paper reproaching the club for failing to invest £70,000 which they had recently received. The Chairman stated that they had money for signings. Buxton said in the press that he was not aware of the available funds. The board responded, claiming that although the manager had been given £80,000 for signings and was always on the phone, he was unable to bring any player in. Following defeat in a cup game, the board sacked Buxton.

While English football is adapting to the Wenger revolution, Alex Calvo García's new manager is famous for breaking a cheekbone of his foreign star.

People are angry. Another letter from a fan to the *Telegraph* asks: 'Do we have to settle for surplus on the balance sheet and free signings of players who are over thirty-five and with low wages? Ambition? Not here!'

Laws knows how to deal with a troublesome dressing room. Three or four players want to leave the club, which was not bringing them the success they want. They dislike the club and avoid work. If the manager is not careful they could take others down the same road. The dressing room is divided in cliques.

Laws has seen it before. He halts the decline. But it is not enough. In his first winter in charge of Scunthorpe he abandons football purism, cherished by him, instilled by Clough. After a 2-0 defeat on a January evening in Macclesfield, at the end of a run of eight defeats, he commands his players to adopt a new philosophy. They will play with a big man up front and a more direct style. Results came. The club misses the play-off by one point. The board renews his contract. He can plan for the next season.

He wants to talk with the Spaniard, who is not bringing enough to the team. Laws reasoning is based on his experience. Players in this division cannot rely on technique and possession of the ball. Two hundred times per match the ball is in no man's land. You have to compete to retrieve a fair percentage of those balls. Alex is not the 'typical Spanish player'. He understands that he needs to be stronger and works in the gym. 'Garsie' has tried to respond to what is required from him, but Laws wants to sign a big striker, John Gayle, who has scored goals at Wembley and wherever else he has been.

The manager wants to speak with 'Alex from Ordizia' but is unable to communicate. Nicola, the Chairman's daughter, acts again as an interpreter. Laws explains that he wants to sign a striker because he does not believe that Alex is the right player. He has scored one goal in all his appearances, a first team regular in November and December but sporadic since. In the Premiership, footballers tend to be intelligent, they have a football brain, but in the Third Division they have less quality and verbal communication is more important.

Calvo García knows it. It has been difficult. The winter was hard, he had never trained on a snow covered field. The supporters have shown great affection to him but some people do not understand who he is, where he comes from. 'Had you seen snow before?' someone asked him.

He feels secluded in a world without values, in a more materialistic society. Players who have left their families when they were sixteen and have lived since then with another family and three or four apprentice footballers, training, playing, cleaning the boots or the shin pads for the masters of the first team. Foreigners are being imported by Premiership clubs and the lower divisions are the last refuge for British players. This is the context. When teams are picked by two players on the training ground, he knows that he will be the last in the queue. Leire went to watch a game in the stand with Alex's team-mates. When she arrived, nobody said a word to her. Back home, players would often go out together with their girlfriends or wives.

Laws knew nothing about Alex. He was a little lost sheep in the dressing room, the quietest person he had ever come across. The Spaniard had technical skills associated with foreigners, he did not smoke or drink, he worked well in training. But he was isolated. He would say 'Good morning' on arrival and no one replied.

A dressing room can be very cruel. Aggressive, abusive, mordant, if the others see you as weak they single you out. You share a closed space during the week, you travel together. Players are ridiculed. There are tears. And your confidence can be emptied when you are the target of constant banter. If an upcoming star buys a new flashy shirt, somebody takes all the buttons out. Or cuts the tips of your socks. Or pours liniment in your shorts. You need a thick skin.

Brian Laws believes that a manager needs to know his players. 'To those with experience and intelligence you do not rant, others need to be shaken. At half time, they carry kicks, bruises and they want to rest. They pretend to be listening but they aren't. And sometimes you provoke an answer by doing something mad like throwing a pot of tea.' This time he has to make a decision about someone who is indecipherable.

The psychologist Laws sits with Alex and Nicola, the interpreter, and he is shocked. He has asked Alex how he has felt about his first season and the mute keeps talking and talking. He believes that the manager is not going to offer him a contract but wants to argue his case. The arrival of spring has left him in awe, he has been jogging on his own, merging happily with the rebirth of nature. Without Leire he would have gone back but they are seeing the light now. He tells the manager that he has never played as a centre forward where Scunthorpe has been playing him. He was an attacking midfielder in Spain. Alex is a good professional and maybe deserves another chance. In the final two matches of the season Laws plays him in midfield. The manager offers him two options: a six months or one year contract. He chooses the second. Alex stays in Scunthorpe.

The most popular literary portrait of Scunthorpe – 'a good place to say goodbye to' – comes from a mobster. Jack Carter returns to the town to avenge the murder of his brother after becoming a prosperous thug among London gangsters.

He takes the train in Euston station and arrives at Doncaster. From there it is a short train journey, looking through the window to the place where he was born.

'At first there's just the blackness. The rocking of the train, the reflections against the raindrops and the blackness. But if you keep looking beyond the reflection you eventually notice the glow creeping into the sky. At first it's slight and you think maybe a haystack or a petrol tanker or something is on fire over a hill and out of sight. But then you notice that the clouds themselves are reflecting the glow and you know that it must be something bigger. And a little later the train passes through a cutting and curves away towards the town, a small bright concentrated area of light and beyond and around the town you can see the causes of the glow, the half-dozen steel works stretching to the rim of the semicircular bowl of hills, flames shooting upwards – soft reds pulsing on the insides of melting shops, white heat sparking in blast furnaces – the structures of the works against the collective glow, all of it looking like a Disney version of the Dawn of Creation.'

Later, when the star of *Get Carter* takes a taxi to go to a pub, he paints Scunthorpe with a broad brush: 'It was a strange place. Too big for a town, too small to be a city. As a kid, it had always struck me that it was like some western boom town. There was just the main street where there was everything you needed and everything else just dribbled off towards the ragged edges of the town.'

In the novel, a director of the football club is a local gangster involved in the murder. Carter shields himself among the crowds leaving a game at the Old Showground to escape the police and many others who are looking for him.

Ted Lewis, author of crime thrillers, lived in nearby Barton-upon-Humber and named his novel 'Jack Carter Returns Home', but the celluloid version was called 'Get Carter'. Michael Caine plays the protagonist, who after the long train ride from London, passes Scunthorpe and into Newcastle. The river Tyne replaces the Humber but the industrial architecture, cobblestone hilly streets, rows of terraced houses, brick, wood and slate, is the necessary backdrop to depict the hard life in the north.

Voyeurs are treated to the beauty of Swedish actress Britt Ekland, muse of 'swinging' London, to embellish a story in which sex is often enforced and cruel. Caine's London accent grates in a character that is supposedly going home. The role of the big villain is played by John Osborne, also a popular dramatist at the time.

Sylvester Stallone played Carter in a Hollywood version, which takes place in Las Vegas and Seattle. Crime is more prosperous in the Stallone film than in Lewis' novel. Golf replaces football, families seem more cohesive, gangsters are computer wizards who chat on cell phones before the kill. Carter sums up his circumstances in absurd dialogue: 'We can't change history, we can't do that, I mean... but we can go past it, just past it'.

In Lewis' novel, neighbouring backdrops like Doncaster or Grimsby are named, but Scunthorpe, where most of the action takes place, is not, although anyone who knows the town can identify its landscape. And the cover of the paperback sets the action in Doncaster.

It is Scunthorpe's misfortune: omitted on some regional maps, left in a geographical limbo between Lincolnshire and South Yorkshire, between the mouth of the Humber and one of its tributaries, the river Trent.

The area lay largely unchanged from the pre-Christian era until the nineteenth century. Acres of flat land, fertile for turnip, wheat, bean or potato. A region invaded by Vikings and forgotten by the British. A sparsely populated and indisposed corner of the kingdom, a landscape of sandy burrows, good for rabbits.

Scunthorpe's famous sons and daughters can be counted on the fingers of one hand: the wife of a famous astronomer, a prominent man of medicine, a great golfer, a world speedway champion. The actress Joan Plowright, wife of Laurence Olivier, was born in the town too.

The romance of Olivier and Plowright echoes as a metaphor for Scunthorpe's place in the sentimental geography of the British. In 1957, Olivier was a world star when he agreed to play the role of Archie Rice in 'The Entertainer', written by the same John Osborne who later played a mobster in 'Get Carter'. Osborne was a member of the generation of angry young men, who in the middle of a post-war economic boom rebelled against a suffocating complacency. They wanted to be relieved of deference and convention. They wanted more honesty. Their anger may also have been tinged with disappointment at their country, which had just lost its empire and was receding into something more provincial and mediocre.

Archie, the protagonist of *The Entertainer*, is a cabaret actor, a womaniser, a drunk and a tax dodger. He sings the tunes of an England no longer believing in itself. Olivier took the role at a time when his career was stagnating. At fifty, his life was drifting towards the marbled stupidity of statues.

His marriage was also in crisis. Those who attended rehearsals of the play, censored by the Lord Chamberlain – 'page 21, delete word 'balls'', said one of his sexually obsessed clips – saw Vivian Leigh crying in her seat illuminated by a ray of light through a window of the Royal Court Theatre. Her husband had just fallen onto his knees playing Archie Rice, dead behind the eyes, perhaps the embodiment of England retreating from Suez.

Archie's daughter, Jean, brings freshness to the stale atmosphere of the family. She has studied and applied herself, deciding not to marry her boyfriend who could not understand why she would attend an anti-war demonstration.

Laurence Olivier left Leigh later while making the film based on the 'The Entertainer'. He began a romance with Jean, played by Joan Plowright, twenty one years younger. Osborne describes Jean as 'dark, with slightly protruding teeth and bad eyesight.'This girl with a rounded and generous mouth, played by the actress from Scunthorpe, should be, according to the script, 'what most people would call plain. Humour and tenderness already beginning to stake their small claim around her nose and eyes.'

Alex and Leire are living in a mill town lacking in notoriety, and with a challenging name. It most likely comes from a man of Scandinavian origin. His name was Skuma and had his farm there. 'Thorpe' derives from Danish. Or maybe, as experts in Norse etymology say, it is a reference to a woman prone to gossip, 'skumur'. Or perhaps it was the name given to black-headed gulls living in the regions' wetlands at the time of the Danes. It was Escumethorp in the Norman census of 1086. In the thirteenth century it had become Scumptorp.

People tend to smile when you say that you are going to Scunthorpe. And there is a degree of paranoia among its inhabitants when someone mentions his interest, as if the only possible purpose of the stranger would be to mock.

Nick Lyons, author of Scunthorpe, *A Photographic History of Your Town*, part of a series of local history books based on the photographic archive of English cities and towns created by Francis Frith, writes: 'As the name of an insignificant hamlet without pretensions to importance, this was acceptable, and no-one noticed. But by the 1930s, when Skuma Thorpe wanted to throw its weight about, people began to show a less than respectful attitude to the name itself. A clergyman who had given good service in the five villages observed in the 1950s that

'Scunthorpe is now a mere name which never fails to raise a laugh on radio or in music hall jest.'

The Anglo-Irish comedian Spike Milligan wrote two books, 'Indefinite Articles and Scunthorpe' and 'Scunthorpe Revisited', in which the mere mention of the name is intended to make people laugh.

The explanation of Lyons is that: 'Allowing that all cultures play with sounds (especially with names) and create stereotypes, we should not be surprised that the hard, unpleasant 'sc' sound, especially followed by 'un' (with the broadest of 'u' sounds), can provoke an admittedly simple-minded mirth. Perhaps Scunthorpe should either learn to live with the response to its name, or look for some appropriate opportunity to change it again.'

Why would anyone laugh on hearing 'scun'? Scunthorpe, with its hard Scandinavian phonetics brings an immediate association with the north of England, a vast region that may be seen as vulgar by people who take themselves to be sophisticated. But that alone is not enough to cause laughter.

Convoluted explanations are offered to avoid the strongest profanity in the English language. What three football teams have a swearword in their name? Scunthorpe, Arsenal and fucking Leeds United.

The word 'cunt' has common roots in medieval Celtic, Nordic, Germanic and Mediterranean languages. It is a sound never to be pronounced in conversation, never published in newspapers, where it is hidden behind grotesque asterisks, c***, never to be broadcast. It may be a quirk in the particular misogyny of the English, less accustomed than the French to say 'con' or the Spaniards profligate use of 'coño'. In *The Vagina Monologues*, American playwright Eve Ensler finally reclaims the word from its prurient reclusion and invites her audiences to chant 'cunt, cunt, cunt...'

The five villages in this part of northern Lincolnshire – Crosby, Scunthorpe, Frodingham, Brumby and Ashby – began to merge as a town council at the beginning of the twentieth century. It was Scunthorpe-Frodingham-Brumby, until a local vicar, Thomas Boughton, a leading member of the Scunthorpe Citizens League, overcame resistance from neighbours in Frodingham, claiming that the name change was a logical outcome of its importance as an ecclesiastical and commercial centre of the region. There already existed a North Frodingham in Yorkshire. Scunthorpe housed most of the population. It was the only one of the five villages that had essential facilities for life in the modern world: a bank, a pharmacy, an off-licence, a fish mongers, money lenders, a cooperative store and a police station. The vicar's campaign, getting signatures, preaching in the streets, did not stop until the unique name of his parish finally prevailed over the 'triple-barrelled monstrosity'.

The feisty vicar and his followers could not foresee that, a century later, filters of obscenity would reject internet searches with the name of their town. The 'Scunthorpe problem' has been used in computing as a generic term for the mistaken blocking of emails, forums posts or searches by overzealous software.

The landscape of the region suffered its first radical change since the time of the Viking invasions with the land enclosures in the first half of the nineteenth century. It was a process of appropriation by the lords of the realm of land on which communal rights had previously existed. This transformation of agriculture is at the origin of industrialisation and capitalism and was somewhat delayed in North Lincolnshire, considering the history of other areas in England.

According to legend, Rowland Winn, later Baron of St Oswald, son of Charles, one of the biggest landowners in the region, invited some friends to a hunt in Frondingham, in 1859. One of them was an entrepreneur of new industries, who noticed the colour and weight of rubbly ironstone extracted by local farmers to kill weeds known as Maidenhair. 'This is iron ore', the guest is supposed to have exclaimed. Winn asked other experts. The discovery of 'ironstone' was confirmed. An industry of opencast mining soon developed, although it was already clear in the early days that extraction in deep mining could be expensive. It would be dangerous due to its low composition in iron and high composition in lime and sulphur.

In February 1875, Winn, descendant of a Welsh draper who served Elizabeth I, enclosed 566 acres of communal lands in the east of Brumby and registered deeds giving him new rights: 'I further declare that I so reserve and set out to the said Lord of the Manor of Brumby (i.e. Charles Winn) all Mines, Minerals, Stone, and other sub-strata under the land to be enclosed, together with a right to enter the said land when enclosed for the purpose of opening, working, or winning such Mines, Minerals, Stone,...'

Labour was needed to extract and load the ore onto the wagons running to the banks of the Trent. Scunthorpe's population in 1851 was 303 people. In the first year of the twentieth century it was 6,750. The five villages gave shelter to 19,678 people in 1911.

Scunthorpe did not prosper from mineral extraction but steel mills. Coal barges arrived. In 1867, there was already a train station, festooned to welcome a triumphant Rowland Winn returning from a court case for the possession of the enclosed land.

Other proprietors sold land to the new council and 'Ironpolis' was born, which brought employees of the mills together under the paternal mantle of the great families, who donated a new town hall, a church, a school, houses.

The train between Doncaster and Scunthorpe runs just like in the times of Jack Carter but the landscape is not as hellish as described by the fictional mobster. The coat of arms has a motto which mirrors Carter's depiction – 'Refulget labores nostros coelo', the heavens reflect our labours – but small mills no longer throw fire to the sky from their furnaces in a pathetic version of the Book of Genesis. After mergers and closures, on the outskirts of the town stands one of the largest steel plants in Britain.

The exploitation of ironstone is long gone and Scunthorpe now benefits from a location, which in ancient times hindered the development of the region. Transport routes by rail and road connect it with the rest of the country and the mouth of the Humber provides deep-water ports.

The Scunthorpe of Alex and Leire is a town of about sixty thousand inhabitants. After the last war, it began to expand over a rolling landscape in a region in which there is no shortage of land to build on. Wide avenues and roads now link the amalgamated districts.

In the town centre there are public buildings, churches, garden centers, pubs, long straight streets lined with rows of houses and cherry trees. There are cricket grounds and rugby pitches.

At the door of the museum, next to the county council building, there is a statue of two soldiers flying an unidentifiable flag with an inscription commemorating the glorious dead of 1914-18. 'To the immortal memory of those from Ironstone who gave their lives for their country.' On the outside wall of the museum a plaque lists those killed in the Second World War, in Korea, the Falklands.

The old main street, which had groceries displaying vegetables, strawberries, tomatoes or beans in wicker baskets, Methodist chapels, florists and tailors, butchers, tobacconists and newsagents, and the headquarters of the powerful cooperative founded by employees of the steelworks, is now a truncated avenue, whose deterioration began in the sixties.

The urban landscape seems broken or incomplete, a typical inner city British town, shaken by the decay of industry and the exacting servitudes to the car in what was a sea of bicycles. High streets that are like photocopies with the same anagrams and colours, the same banks, the same chemists and discount stores, shopping centres with identical and unimaginative architecture. The Victoria and Albert Museum acquired in 2004 a thirty-five-year-old postcard of the commercial road of Scunthorpe, part of a collection of boring postcards by Martin Parr, a photographer renowned for his artistic portrayal of everyday life.

There are Indian, Italian and Thai restaurants, a German bar, a café or two and several pubs, fast food joints. Some premises are empty. At the end of the street, the shopping malls and, next to the library and leisure center, the bus station and an ugly multi-storey car park. In the library there are notices from associations of parents of children with disabilities or from people who care for family or friends, offers of courses on gardening or meditation, a request to form a group of writers to exchange ideas or review their creations. Another group, called The Readers, meet in pubs or private homes to discuss their favourite writers and go together to the theatre, cinema or literary festivals. There is a support group for job seekers on how to write application letters or CVs. On the shelves, the library is well stocked and with books in Hindi, Gujarati, Punjabi, Urdu or Bang.

Beyond the library, to the east, there is a neighbourhood with three tall tower blocks, the only high rise buildings of the town. From there the striking silhouette of the steelworks can be seen as backdrop to the Church of St. John, given to the town by the Winns, built in the Gothic Revival style that became popular in the Victorian era at the centre of what was then a lively district of commercial buildings and housing. The church, now isolated, is a museum of contemporary art.

The first pictures of the town show the solemn architecture of The Conservative and The Liberal clubs. But since 1935, when a builder, John Quibell, seized political representation of the district in

Westminster, the town elected Labour members of parliament, which also held control the council.

Alex spends his first lonely afternoons in the snooker hall next to Britannia corner, alongside pubs, gardens encircled by traffic, takeaways promising culinary instant satisfaction, derelict churches and the old public baths.

When Leire arrives she finds work in a hospital. They buy a house in Bottesford, a suburb with front and back gardens. Alex enrolls at the Open University to study communication and information technology. Scunthorpe is a good place to raise children, a comfortable town for people enjoying family life, friends, television.

Life is now rewarding and happy. Work and play, trips to surrounding towns like Brigg and Epworth, which maintain their old market town centres, visits to stately homes and gardens open to the public, to farms that sell their goods at harvest time for those who come for tea and homemade cake. On weekends they visit antique markets on abandoned British air force bases around Lincolnshire. Leeds, Sheffield or York are all within a short drive down the motorway.

The steely town of 'Get Carter' is not the only literary portrait of Scunthorpe. Stephen Benatar had already composed in *Wish Her Safe At Home* a great character of English literature in the end of the twentieth century- the theatrical spinster Rachel Waring-, when he wrote *Such Men Are Dangerous*, set in Scunthorpe.

His protagonist, Simon Madison, keen on ping pong, is living through his own doubts and dreams as vicar of St. Matthews when an angel appears to the two sons of a lady devoted to his church, telling them that the world is heading for disaster.

The vicar and his mother, who have come from Bournemouth, are aware of the constraints of life in a town where finding a good job in the mid-eighties was, indeed, a miracle, and where there is not a single bookshop. They resent the stereotypes but why on earth should an angel now choose Scunthorpe to deliver God's message, wonders Simon.

'Scunthorpe of all places! The very name was a music hall joke; the easy butt of every second-rate comedian. Simon had become genuinely fond of the town over the past three years and was often vociferously indignant at the rotten press that it received; but the fact remained that Scunthorpe was not a spot that the British media, or indeed the British population at large, in general treated seriously'.

If God's angel tells the children of 'Such Men Are Dangeorus' that the world is heading for disaster, the choice of Scunthorpe may have been appropriate because the truncated town and its lifestyle – visitors arriving from the west are greeted by a road sign, 'Welcome to Scunthorpe, Industrial Garden Town' – is what remains of a dream of collective harmony devised by Ebenezer Howard.

To-morrow, A Peaceful Path to Real Reform, a book of 167 pages published by Howard in 1898, is the political manifesto of a man who had already invented a shorthand typewriter. Howard was knighted for his plans to build new garden cities, his way to solve the conflict between capitalism and communism at a time of social unrest in British cities, especially in London.

Howard's vision was a municipal co-operativism, a country of 'social cities' that would allow the reconstruction of harmony broken by massive migration of rural populations in search of the promises of industry.

Howard's strategy was cautious but his utopian yearning is clear in the introduction to his book: 'The key to the problem how to restore the people to the land — that beautiful land of ours, with its canopy of sky, the air that blows upon it, the sun that warms it, the rain and dew that moisten it — the very embodiment of Divine love for man — is indeed a Master-Key, for it is the key to a portal through which, even when scarce ajar, will be seen to pour a flood of light on the problems of intemperance, of excessive toil, of restless anxiety, of grinding poverty, over the limits of Governmental interference and even the relations of man to the Supreme Power.'

Howard was not a great writer and, although he expressed lyricism about the fertility of land, neither was he a good farmer. At twenty years of age, he left England to settle down in Nebraska. But he had to move to Chicago to make a living as a stenographer in a law firm.

At twenty six, he returned to London, where he found work as a copyist in parliament and became familiar with the great debates of his time. He was educated in the religion of dissenters unwilling to recognise ecclesiastical hierarchy. He attended Congregationalist services, communities gathered around a shared reading of the Bible.

His nonconformist background led him to sympathise with movements of land socialism, of common ownership of water or gas. But Howard concluded that socialism was not the answer to the problems of the world as it dispensed with the impulses of the individual. He sympathised with the writings of a Russian exile, Prince Peter Kropotkin, advocating an anarchist communism concerned with the organisation of local life.

Howard designed in *To-Morrow* a new town of thirty thousand inhabitants, with a central park and a crystal palace, a square for trade, ways for rapid communication, homes, health centres, areas reserved for industry and an outer ring dedicated to agriculture and livestock.

The garden town would be built through the acquisition of 2,500 acres of agricultural land by mortgage debentures and then legally vested in the names of 'four gentlemen of responsible position and of undoubted probity and honour.' The start of construction of the new town would increase the price of the purchased land. The local community would accumulate an initial capital that would be used to repay the loan, so that a reasonable fee would be sufficient for the municipal services.

'To-Morrow' is the book of a man wanting to convince others to develop his project and therefore looks into every detail that would challenge its viability. It combines the pursuit of perfection - 'a town, like a flower, or a tree, or an animal, should, at each stage of its growth, possess unity, symmetry, completeness' - with detailed suggestions on how to solve world dilemmas.

For example, in regards to the problem of unnecessary competition between stores selling the same goods, Howard proposes a 'local option'. A garden town council would rent a shop with the assurance that another tenant would not be granted another license of the same type, but if a number of neighbours complain about the way in which the shopkeeper trades, the council will permit the opening of an 'opposition shop' and allow competition.

This complicity of residents, committed to the maintenance of their community and its cooperative principle, would have 'the power of dealing in the most drastic manner possible with the liquor traffic.' Such is his horror at the plague of alcoholism in large urban areas that, since moderate drinkers cannot be punished with prohibition, all taxes from the sale of alcoholic drinks should be devoted to compete with that trade.

Ebenezer Howard wanted to live amongst happy and honourable people. He also saw the advantages of sport. In a section that details everything the resident would receive for his investment, swimming baths are included. A large area of the Central Park should be 'reserved for cricket fields, lawn-tennis courts and other recreation grounds'. Perhaps the new game of football did not fit into the ideal society. Perhaps the parliamentary stenographer only liked the summer games of the elegant people.

Four years after the publication of 'To-morrow', Quakers who sympathised with Howard's ideas built Letchworth. Other garden towns were built later, and after World War II, a movement for the construction of new towns tried to apply his ideas to palliate the problems of congestion and degradation in urban life. But these new towns had little to do with the original design. Instead of land condominiums promoted by associations of citizens, they were promoted by the state. Nothing survived in these new towns of the municipal government devised by Howard.

The green belt and the introduction of nature in the urban fabric remains a feature of town planning. But the ideal of a network of towns based on a cooperative society proposed by Howard to solve conflicts in the modern world transformed in Scunthorpe as in every other town and city into a private ambition of owning a house with a garden in a suburban sprawl.

It is a mid-table match, one of the games clogging United's calendar due to postponements over the long winter.

'Iron! Iron! Iron!'

The Doncaster Road End fans are singing on a cold and windy evening. It does not take them long to warm up.

Striker Steve MacLean goes down in the Kidderminster Harriers box but the referee ignores the penalty shouts. The crowd is angry. MacLean looks to the sidelines, where Laws unhappily watches.

'I have to be very careful on what I say about the referee,' he tells reporters afterwards. 'He was the referee here when we played Hull City and he said after that game that he thought he made a mistake when he gave us a penalty because Steve MacLean had actually dived. I knew and even said before kick-off that he wasn't going to give anything if Steve was fouled. It's disgusting from a referee's point of view to say what he did and be so blasé about it. What he did from a refereeing perspective is disgusting. It's unprofessional but he'll be all right because he'll have gone and had a good night's sleep. Steve could have broken his leg or had his head chopped off and he still wouldn't have given it.'

The Iron are better in the first few minutes but they soon go back to the pattern of launching long balls to Steve Torpey in hope that something would happen. The visitors have settled. They are fast coming forward. A veteran of these divisions, Mark Yates, plays well in front of their defence, moving forward with intelligence and danger.

In the 18th minute they attack again down the right. Yates gets into the area and his low shot is palmed away by keeper Tommy Evans. The ball is loose and an opposition forward gets to it before his marker Nathan Stanton.

'I think Stanton was on Planet Zog', says Brian Laws post-match, referring to his captain. 'He certainly wasn't on Planet Earth. The job he had to do was a basic sweeping-up job for a full back, but he was asleep.'

Scunthorpe play without conviction for the rest of the first half. Entertainment is found in the stands. Evans runs from goal to throw a quick ball but he stops when realising that his target is being marked. A fan chides him. The goalkeeper turns round.

'Fuck off!'

The fans find it hilarious. They sing 'There's only one Tommy Evans' and then point to the traitor: 'You're a wanker!'

The goalkeeper of Scunthorpe might enlighten the supporters with his sober thoughts when talking about his career. 'Where you are is as good as you are. If you were better you would not be here.' He had a plan: three years in the Third Division, two in the Second Division,… But it did not work that way.

Later, more groans are directed at Evans when he runs again to throw the ball early but finds nobody available. The crowd were excited and then disappointed, and finally happy when Evans punts a high ball for Steve Torpey to continue his perennial air combat with the enemy.

In the second half, Scunthorpe play better until a visitors' apparently innocuous attack ends with a volley flying into the net. The joy of the hundred from Kidderminster is heard and the silent frustration of the two thousand five hundred from Scunthorpe can be felt. The game is agony until the final whistle. The Harriers block Taylor and Beagrie crossing balls from the wings. They force them to go inside, where there is a compact thread of players. They play with a deep defence to leave less space behind and Scunthorpe have no variety in their game.

When an overly zealous tackle from Kevin Sharp on a Kidderminster player stops a counterattack, the recipient reacts angrily and Sharp kicks him. Sharp is sent off. The Iron are two goals down and now play with ten men.

'We have a code of conduct here that needs to be adhered to,' Laws tells reporters after the match. 'You can't retaliate, end of story. All right, he's lost the ball and the lad's kicked him, but he's kicked him back and if the referee *has seen it's a red card. Sharp knows that if you kick a rival, you will be sent off. Now he'll get hurt in his pocket and possibly lose his place in the side. But there's only one person he can scream and shout at and that's himself.'*

Scunthorpe is a boxer getting hammered in the ring, hoping that the damage is not fatal before it is time to return home.

'I agree with the fans,' says the manager. 'I cannot accept this type of performance. Everyone has been atrocious. Not being able to play well at Glanford Park is inexplicable. Players are given all the information necessary to do their jobs. They must know that this kind of thing affects their contracts and their salaries. During the break I told them they had to increase the pace and, after telling them, they acted like they did not want to play.'

Jan Molby, coach of Kidderminster Harriers, goes home happy. He is Danish, schooled at Ajax of Amsterdam, in the more democratic football of Nordic Europeans and Ducth, where players discuss tactics with their coaches. He arrived in Liverpool in 1984.

He was a heavy and unhurried footballer. The fans composed songs to celebrate his weight and his virtues: 'He is fat / he is round / his arse is on the ground / Jan Molby! Jan Molby!' When he began his coaching career, the secretary of Rhayader, a Welsh club, offered him through the press a contract with a salary in meat. Some of the club directors were farmers.

But he commandeered the FA Cup final in 1986 against Everton. Majestic and beefy, brain, belly and boot, maybe some music, a ballet for men, a varied and exact distribution of passing, long and short, always to feet.

Molby was leaving Glanford Park with a victory that distanced his club from relegation. His team had played with speed and control: 'I'm trying to change the culture and the key is patience. Players must learn to pass and move. But, if you try to change the style, you have trouble with the fans, they get nervous because they want on-your-face football. In other European leagues, football is like a chess game, but here they like the physical game. It's changing under the influence of foreign players and coaches. While playing for Liverpool, they told me that I was slow, that I was not aggressive, but I felt comfortable because I was tactically superior. Aggressiveness and anticipation are different things.'

'I knew Steve Torpey when I was at Swansea,' says Molby. 'Scunthorpe play through him but I do not want static centre-forwards, I want movement and speed.'

While Scunthorpe are plunged into a crisis, which is compounded by public criticism of his players by their manager, the Harriers coach travels home sharing the amazement of foreigners about the persistence by those who created the game to use tactics that make no sense. But Molby likes to be part of it: 'I try to change the way the game is played but I like the passion, what football means to people. Where else could you find this atmosphere? What other country has ninety-two professional clubs and fans who are willing to die for the club? This is the only place.'

It is 8:30, 20 March 2004, and we are in a car at Britannia corner, listening to the radio.

Radio Humberside has a correspondent at the Vetch Field, waiting for the match referee to inspect the pitch. Some kind of hurricane blew across the country yesterday with strong winds and torrential rain.

While the referee and his assistants conduct their inspection, the radio station entertains us with a quiz.

'Which Prime Minister said that 'we have never had it so good' and made a speech about 'the winds of change'?'

John Staff, Scunthorpe United historian, answers correctly.

'Harold Macmillan.'

The contestant fails.

The referee has finished his stroll around the pitch and tells the correspondent that the game will be played.

'Ground staff have assured me that they can drain the puddles and the wind will help.'

We can set off.

A hundred or so Scunthorpe fans travelled to Torquay recently, 300 miles there and 300 miles back, only to find when they reached the South coast that the match had been postponed.

Torquay is the furthest town in the Fourth Division from Scunthorpe. At 270 miles, Swansea is second. Tuesday's loss against Kidderminster has left a bad taste and only the utterly faithful make the trip. Five had registered for the supporters coach, it was cancelled. This time we have to go by car.

John Staff is in no doubt.

'Of course we are mad. No matter whether it snows, rains or it is a good day, we support from the stands.'

Jerry Mahony is our driver and also the team's mascot, the Scunny Bunny kicking balls at Hull with apparent reluctance. Everything has an explanation. Jerry suffers from Wilson's disease, a genetic, degenerative disorder, which affects the nervous system. It is difficult to understand what he says but he is a good man and a good driver.

The other traveller is Jack, aged seventeen, working as an apprentice carpenter in Sheffield. This year he has been at every game. He does not play football. He follows Manchester United but he draws a distinction between being a fan of a team and being a follower. When you follow a team, you watch the games on TV and you look for the results. When you are a fan, you travel over 500 miles on a blustery Saturday, proudly wearing the club's shirt just to watch a team that is playing poorly.

Spring is just around the corner but we traverse an England of trees with bare branches, low grey skies, oppressive humidity, gales and rain. Motorway signs announce the imminence of Sherwood Forest, where Robin Hood was said to take cover, the Derbyshire Dales, which inspired Jane Austin or Charlotte Bronte, the magnificent Chatsworth House.

Fans in other colours speed past. Those with blue and white scarves flapping against the window of a car travelling in the opposite direction, who are they?

Jerry has a CD with a music collection from the last Rugby World Cup: the rock operetta of Queen, the tenderness of Cyndi Lauper singing 'True Colours', the tribal 'Haka' of the New Zealand All Blacks, a horrible electronic version of Jerusalem.

We stop at a motorway service station selling sandwiches and tea, chicken, roast beef, sausages, baked beans, but the Scunthorpe crew have brought food from home. We go to the toilet and depart. In each urinal, at eye level, an advert suggests a remedy against erectile dysfunction.

We reach Wales. We cross the rolling landscape of Monmouthshire, signs that point us in the direction of Cardiff or the Rhondda Valley, towards places where industrialisation has been reversed and harbours are now for recreation, where old mining valleys are now covered in lush green grass.

The motorway reveals the outline of the Port Talbot steelworks, sister to Scunthorpe's. The car's occupants count three furnaces, one less than at home. We arrive an hour and a quarter before kick-off to a shopping mall car park and pull up next to a windswept beach.

Vetch Field, which was the kingdom of John Toshack and will be demolished when the season finishes, has the flavour of old football. The first pitch made out of clinker, in 1912, was set on the grounds of a disused coal store that had been built on a field of local cabbage. It is embedded in a terraced neighbourhood, next to a prison.

Walking around the ground to find the club shop, where Jerry has to swap some programmes, we see open alleyways between houses leading to the stadium and a metal arch which tells us that this is the players, referees, managers and press entrance.

In front of the club shop there is a pub, in which men station themselves outside drinking beer and looking to catch the eyes of rival fans. It is not yet the time to sing about their home: 'I'll stand here on the North Bank until the day I die/ Take me to the Vetch Field, way down by the sea/ where I will follow Swansea, Swansea City.'

The latrines in the visitors stand are in a concrete hut, with a canal cut through the floor, where there are some yellow balls of disinfectant. A man coming out of the urinal makes his point.

'Nice, huh?'

The booth that sells sausages and tea is separated from the visitors by a metal grid. Tea is requested through a square hole cut thirty by thirty centimetres. There is a counter, separated a metre from the grid. A young woman stretches her arm out to deliver tea to the customer, who has then to put his arm through another square in order to get to the milk and a plastic stick to stir this tea behind bars.

There are fifty four Scunthorpe fans. The man from Ashford, in southeast London, who travels every Saturday to see the Iron play, no matter where. The Blue Bell barman and Andy, who works in a bank and stands in the Doncaster Road End at Glanford Park. And Margaret and her friend Kate, who never miss a match. Margaret is upset with Brian Laws.

'The last time we played like Tuesday the manager was fired. He should not criticise the players on the radio. These things have to be kept in the dressing room.'

Her husband is not interested in football. She went with her older sister to the Old Showground when she was thirteen and found the whole thing exhilarating.

'Iron! Iron!'

There is applause for Tommy Evans when he reaches his goal. But Margaret is not optimistic: 'I do not like this referee. When we played at Rochdale, he sent our goalkeeper off for catching the ball outside the area, but he was inside.'

Football is a game that commences at three o'clock in the afternoon on an English Saturday.

The first ball of the match is depressing. Pass backwards and then a big lump forward which ends in the hands of the rival goalkeeper.

Less than half an hour into the game and Scunthorpe combine well on the left and the Welsh defence are unbalanced. Cleveland Taylor is left unmarked on the right.

A young boy celebrates the goal by opening his arms and screaming at the Swansea fans, who are a hundred feet away.

'The Welsh are bastards!'

Two stewards glare at the visitor with sullen eyes.

'Cleveland! Cleveland!'

The supporters cheer Taylor's feat, he dodges his team-mates and races to hug his manager.

Gradually Swansea gain possession. In midfield they have Roberto Martínez, team captain, one of the 'Three Amigos' of Wigan, the one who stayed when the others left. He has had two injuries this season but still shows the best football brain amongst those gathered in Vetch Field on this inclement afternoon.

He makes himself available to receive the ball from his defence, reads the flow of the game to get into positions that would allow him to intercept the enemy advance and regain possession. When he has the ball, he distributes it well, always to a team-mate, gaining ground by patience and looking for the one-two or the longer pass behind the defence. Talking continuously, marking the lines of containment and pressure, aiming to keep the team as a compact unit.

A high ball into the box and one of Laws' beleaguered players pushes an opponent. A penalty is given. All square. When the locals' euphoria wanes, a children's choir perseveres. They sit together and against the hurricane sing the sweet name of their tribe.

Kate says at half-time that she would settle for a draw. Margaret is complaining about the referee again.

'I like to feel part of a group', she says. 'And I like to follow the team of my town, which is a small team, so everything is more friendly. It's not the same if you follow Manchester United. I like to feel part of a unique experience.'

In the second half, the Scunthorpe defence quickly chills even the most passionate fan. In the 70th minute the score is 4-1. Nobody on the pitch looks interested. Laws makes his substitutions. Disorder, integral part to the entire human experience, defines this Scunthorpe. We are mere samples of a grand reality.

The Welsh joy degenerates into revenge. When Ridley handles the ball on the edge of the area, home fans sing.

'Same old English, always cheating.'

The bitterness turns into celebration and songs of victory.

'Swansea till I die. I'm Swansea till I die.'

With just five minutes to go, there is a goal mouth scramble and Taylor nets a loose ball. He doesn't celebrate the goal, expecting perhaps that the referee would blow for offside. The goal is given, 4-2, and there is a late and humorous applause from the fans.

On the way back, radio voices crush the monotony of mileage. We listen to the commentary of the second half of England versus Wales in the Six Nations rugby tournament and of Newcastle-Charlton. Then to a fans phone-in about the day's games. A supporter expresses his sympathy to the family of a teenager from Everton, who has died in Leicester when he was hit by flying debris. Followed by someone complaining about a referee.

Occasionally the BBC gets their cricket correspondent on the line, who speaks in an English sculpted at a public school. He chronicles the efforts of the two English batsmen in the Queen's Park Oval, in Port of Spain, who have stabilised their innings after the quick removal of the opening pair in the morning session. They are able to resist, even though the umpires have left them to the mercy of aggressive Caribbean bowlers under what the correspondent describes as murky light.

The motorways of England have fallen into darkness. In the services where we stop on the way back, the same ads recommend the same erection remedies.

Tired of the radio, we play a game of questions and answers.

'*Which United player scored goals in the league and in all the cups last year?*', asks Jerry.

'*Steve Torpey*', responds Jack.

John Staff, employee of the steelworks, who dedicates his free time tracing the history of steam locomotives, his family and football clubs, preferably of those that have disappeared, explains the memorabilia market. In the latest catalogue he ordered, you can bid for a program from the founders of Manchester United with a starting price of three thousand pounds. He now seeks Scunthorpe programmes from the 1955-56 season. His knowledge is impressive and he enthusiastically recalls the dates and names of football in the origins of the league.

It is quarter past ten in the evening when we get home. John usually goes with his wife to a pub where the owner allows patrons to drink their pints on a Saturday beyond the closing time. Jack goes home to watch the highlights of the day's matches. Jerry goes to work at a nightclub until two in the morning.

Spring is not reaching Glanford Park. On a cold night, bottom of the division Carlisle are the visitors. They play better in the opening minutes and their supporters are in a good voice. The Telegraph reports that Brian Laws has the backing of the Board, an unmistakable sign that it has considered firing him.

Alex Calvo García, who is now a regular writer of football columns in the pages of the local paper, is on the bench, after four months recovering from his injury. When his name is delivered by the PA system, the fans chant the English version of his name.

'*García! García! García!*'

The visitors easily find their way into the area. Scunthorpe seem dazed. There is no pace, no anticipation, no aggressiveness. Before the 15th minute they fall behind. The cries of 'United, United' have now vanished. Silence and introspection.

Brian Laws' barmy army reacts. They are playing now with higher tempo. Taylor scores before the end of the first half.

After the break, the Iron start the livelier. A Carlisle counter-attack and another goal. Fans run onto the pitch to celebrate. A steward tackles one of them before he can get back to the stand. Delight echoes from the locals, who sing to him their goodbyes.

'It's nice to know you're here, it's nice to know you're here, it's nice to know you're here. Now fuck off!'

Taylor gets into the box. Penalty. MacLean scores. The spirits are lifted. United. United.

But there is an attacking move at the other end and a strong black player, who has been running the whole field during the game, scores a great goal from outside the area.

Carlisle resist until the end.

'We want 'García'. We want 'García', chant a group in the terrace.

But no one can remedy the problems in this team. They are disjointed, lacking in energy or intelligence.

Yet again, Scunthorpe had a dreadful second half. Their rivals appear to be fitter.

'Fuck off Lawsy, Fuck off Lawsy.'

The crowd has turned against the manager.

A group of fans preserve their sense of humour.

'We're going down to the Conference. Down to the Conference. We're going down to the Conference.'

And when the referee blows full time, some of the fans approach the railing in the hope that the manager can see them and hear their contempt.

'Walk out. Walk out.'

Brian Laws impassively defies their repudiation and walks onto the pitch to congratulate his players one by one when they march with their heads down to the tunnel. They have won three of the last nineteen games.

In the intensely cold night, supporters of Scunthorpe United Football Club walk back to their homes. They are orderly people, quietly conversing. They give way to strangers in the clumsy manoeuvring of the crowd and hope for a better future.

It happened one day after the Carlisle defeat.
Brian Laws was sacked on a Wednesday, at the end of March. According to the Telegraph, last week the board had given him a month to improve results. But the deadline had been amended three days later.

People express outrage on Internet forums. No one understands why the board fired a coach with only eight games remaining. If the team gets dragged into the relegation battle, the Board will look like a bunch of fools, and Laws, a sacrificial lamb.

The appointment of Russ Wilcox is announced, working alongside the team physiotherapist Nigel Adkins and youth coach Paul Wilson. Wilcox came to Scunthorpe as a central defender signed by Laws, who later named him as his assistant.

The atmosphere is chilly at Glanford Park on Saturday afternoon. Wilcox's first Scunthorpe team faces Leyton Orient, who have nothing to play for.

The new manager acknowledges the fans when his name is heard over the loudspeakers and met with applause; he then shakes hands with all the players.

Calvo García is not on the bench. Wilcox does not want to be swayed by sympathy towards the legend and be forced to bring him on as a substitute.

Perhaps Scunthorpe's pace is slightly faster at the beginning than in the last few games. They score the goal that gives hope to a new era, then Orient equalise in the second half. The team noticeably struggles. Statistics show that Scunthorpe have been easy prey in the closing minutes of games. The new boss cannot sort out the fitness of the team overnight.

The match ends in a draw, but the other clubs struggling at the bottom have fared worse and Scunthorpe are safe.

Scunthorpe United Football Club is a creation of Methodist Christians. Its founders and its most influential secretary, Harry Allcock, were followers of the religious path outlined by the Wesley brothers.

They were born in the eighteenth century, in Epworth, a few miles from Scunthorpe. The church where their father was vicar still remains, as well as the house where the brothers and sisters were born and educated by their mother, Susanne.

In the Wesley household, faith was restless while the mother attended to the needs of an endless offspring. She only lapsed from pregnancy or labour when the theological quarrels with her husband pulled them apart. She bore eighteen or nineteen children, of which ten survived.

Susanne and Samuel Wesley came from families of London dissenters. Political and religious strife caused large migrations of nonconformists to America, where they founded their ideal communities, but Wesley remained in England, serving the Church headed by the monarch. Susanne did not accept the reigns of William III and Mary II and though husband and wife shared the High Church communion of the time, it was not enough to dampen their disputes about doctrine. Samuel left for a few months, his farewell becoming a gem for dictionaries of quotes: 'We must part for if we have two kings we must have two beds.'

Susanne did not accept the teachings of the new preacher sent to Epworth and held meetings at his house with her children, friends and servants. These prayer sessions and Bible readings made her suspect of running a conventicle, an inadmissible heterodoxy.

She was a ferocious worker. Tour guides today at Epworth Old Rectory, a place of pilgrimage for Methodists worldwide, explain in the kitchen, that the method applied by Susanne Wesley there to educate her children, each on specific days of the week, and to govern her family, is the origin of Methodism.

There were other influences: the mystical revelations experienced by the Wesley brothers, which coincided with heart palpitations; their time in Oxford and the 'Holy Club'; their disappointing experience among the Indians of Georgia, from where they returned after having a few brushes with the authorities, and impressed by the piety of Moravian emigrants, who had weathered the stormy seas with a serenity that the brothers had wished for themselves.

At thirty years of age, the eldest brother, John, pursued the love of an eighteen-year old and at thirty-seven a woman of twenty-three. Finally, he settled for an unhappy marriage with a wealthy widow, Mary Vazeille, who left him, causing her husband's morose verdict: 'Non eam reliqui, non dimissi, non revocabo', 'I did not leave her, I did not send her away, I will not call her back.' Charles, the youngest, married at forty a woman of twenty.

Methodism, founded by the Wesleys as an evangelical revival movement within the Church of England, ended up being a separate church. It is associated with the emergence of the socialist movement, although among its followers notable conservatives like Margaret Thatcher or George W. Bush can be counted.

The brothers toured the British Isles on horseback to preach in public to audiences of two or three thousand people and extended a network of small groups. Those who did not fulfil the requirements for Christian perfection were purged. Drinkers of alcohol were expelled as well as those who had public disputes, gossiped about other people, failed to behave honestly in their business or cheated on their taxes. Methodists were known as 'the singers', because their followers often sang hymns published by the brothers. Charles wrote about six and a half thousand psalms during his lifetime.

The passion and rigour of the Wesley brothers took root in Scunthorpe with a growing population attracted to the steel industry. And those who wanted to instill among the young Christians the muscular virtues of sport created football clubs.

Scunthorpe United took to the field in its first game in the Midlands league at Elland Road to play against Leeds City reserves. Dressed in claret and blue, they were emulating one of the best teams of that era, Aston Villa, also born under the auspices of a Methodist chapel.

Bob Steels begins his history of the club with this sentence: 'Life has almost always been a struggle for Scunthorpe United since it was formed as a professional club in 1910.' The Protestant ethic of life as an exacting endeavour exists in the football club as a persistent ambition to rise from the mediocrity of regional leagues to victory among the great, something resembling glory.

Its history between 1910 and 1950 accounts for that effort. The management is prudent, professionals are signed, but without ever failing to balance the books. The devout Allcock, organizer of Sunday schools and clubs, was secretary from 1914.

In the list of players in the twenties, there is a defensive partnership, Bullivant and Robinson, deserving to be high on a ranking of classical sounding pairings. Sheffield United paid a thousand pounds for the services of left winger Fred Tunstall, who became an England international. Ernie Simms, who had played one match for England, was a surprise signing in 1926.

The chapter on the decade before the Second World War, in the club's history written by John Staff, carries the title *Striving for More Perfection*. Echoes of Wesleyan verse. The chronicle is peppered with recurring emotions. A terrible loss, 3-9, at Christmas, 1933, against close rivals Grimsby Town, and the lack of goals in subsequent matches elicits caustic comments from the 'tough steel workers', who contemplate the fall into 'the abyss of mediocrity in the middle of the table.'

Three years later, the club contracted their first manager, Tom Crilly, who also played in defence, but after two grey seasons he was made redundant. The club returns to the proven methods of a meeting between players and administrators to decide the line-up, combined with the provision by the secretary of prompt information by hanging the results of other matches on the dressing room door.

The club had the ambition to enter the Football League. The steelworks was doing well, gate receipts were good. Allcock trusts a former Welsh international, Tom Jones, who had played for Manchester United, to take over as manager. Scunthorpe wins the Midlands League and travels to London to seek membership in the Football League, but they are rejected.

The war interrupted everything. Some players are enlisted, the league only survived for a few months. Neighbouring Grimsby Town, who were richer but could not play in their ground due to restrictions on the concentration of people in coastal towns, asked if they could use the Old Showground. In 1942, they played against Sunderland in front of twelve thousand spectators in the War Cup, while the Luftwaffe flew over the region, targeting the RAF Dambusters, which were sent to bombard the dams in the valley of the river Ruhr, aiming to flood the industrial infrastructure of Germany.

Eight years later, Scunthorpe United Football Club was finally admitted to the Third Division North. They entered a competition in which promotion and relegation were not dependent any more on league administrators pondering the economic health of the aspiring club but on results on the field. The father of Joan Plowright, the actress who married Laurence Olivier, led the successful delegation. The board stated that to consolidate the club in this new category they would need fifteen thousand fans at every home game, in a town of fifty thousand.

The name, Scunthorpe and Lindsey United, was simplified and they were given the nickname 'Knuts', a derivation of nuts, coined by a subtle commentator that saw the team as a tough nut to crack. At the start of the 1950/51 season, fifty years after the club had been formed, the nickname of 'The Iron' was adopted.

National football brought big teams to the Old Showground, especially in the cups. Alf Ramsey and Sir Stanley Matthews played there. Brian Clough, then Middlesbrough striker, scored three goals in each of the matches against United in the 1958/59 season, after the Iron had reached the Second Division.

The FA Cup match against Sunderland at Roker Park was watched by 56,507 spectators but football was not attracting crowds as big as it had at the turn of the century. Something was happening. When the club was on the brink of promotion to the First Division in 1962, the average attendance was 9,657 spectators, when just a few years before, big games attracted twice that number. Matches were moved to Friday evenings, yet nothing could bring back the good times. Did the popularity of television cause the drop in spectators, who now preferred to be entertained in their living rooms?

How can such a fall in attendance be explained when Scunthorpe had Barry Thomas, their best ever striker? And alongside Thomas played Peter 'Bin-man' Donnelly, who practised his shooting against a goal made out of two rubbish bins. When the team returned to the Third Division, which was no longer divided into two geographical groups of north and south, the club recorded, in the spring of 1965, the lowest ever attendance, 2,755 spectators. Three years later they were in the Fourth Division.

The club that signed Alex Calvo García did not offer its new players a trip around the trophy room to impress them. But the people of Scunthorpe remembered. The promotion of 1972. Relegation in 1973. That game in the FA Cup against Newcastle. The crisis of 1982, when the club was on the brink of extinction due to financial problems. Selling the Old Showground to a supermarket chain ensured survival and allowed the construction of a new stadium in a cornfield in Glanford, outside the town boundaries.

It was a sensible and forward-thinking club, the first to construct a new purpose-built stadium in English football since the fifties. It was opened by Princess Alexandra. Margaret Thatcher, born in nearby Grantham, came to bless such modernity, which presumably would put an end to the football tragedies tarnishing her zealous leadership. A stand had burned down at Bradford killing 56 people. Change had to come. It was the end of gregariousness in old wooden stands, filled with men smoking, drinking, shouting obscenities, sometimes fighting, packed to the rafters, where children were lovingly passed above heads towards the front rows. This was the old Britannia, which the Methodist Thatcher wanted to convert to her cleansing creed.

The club that signed Calvo García had a stadium with a capacity for ten thousand spectators, did its training in various pastures around the town and whose fans remembered. The promotion of 1982. Relegation in 1983. The free-scoring strike partnership of Daws and Flounders. The days of Ian Botham, who later captained the England cricket team. And that trip, on 23 May, 1992, to Wembley Stadium.

The Football League had established a beautiful and absurd method of settling promotion between divisions. The top two or three teams are promoted directly to the higher league and the next four compete in two semi-finals, whose winners vie for promotion at Wembley Stadium. While teams in the top are content with going up, those fighting just below get the chance to achieve one of the most joyous experiences a footballer can have. Scunthorpe went to Wembley in 1992 and lost in a penalty shoot-out.

Defeat at Wembley. The promotions. The relegations. The hope each year that the cup will draw the club against one of the big teams.

The hope each year of escaping what the club chronicler John Staff called 'the abyss of mediocrity'.

In January 1999, Scunthorpe manager, Brian Laws, wrote an article in the *Telegraph* about the influence of foreigners in English football. Seven years before, there had been ten foreign players in the top division and now there were over two hundred.

Laws had worn 'Garibaldi red' at Nottingham Forest, a colour adopted by the founders of the club impressed by the military tactics and charisma of the Italian statesman, who became popular in England after his visit in 1864. But Clough called the Italians 'cheating fucking Italian bastards' after a defeat in Turin and Laws had lost his previous job at Grimsby precisely for having a fight with an Italian. And in his last months at Forest, he had played with a Norwegian, Lars Bohinen, who, after moving to another club, made derogatory comments about Nottingham.

Laws had shared the dressing room with the Dutchman, Bryan Roy, a subtle though somewhat lethargic left winger or centre forward. In that year, 1999, when he wrote his article, another Dutchman, Johannes Petrus Ferdinandus 'Pierre' van Hooijdonk, went on strike in protest at the lack of summer signings by Forest, which had been promoted the previous season thanks largely to his goals.

'It's the money that has attracted the top foreign stars to this country and that has prompted 'Gazza' to claim that too many have flooded into our game', wrote Laws. 'At the moment there must be an average of about 10 foreign players on the books of each Premier League club. The one exception is Aston Villa - and good luck to them'.

'One thing so many foreign players have done I believe is take some of the passion out of our game. They are all right when things are going well, but too many of them duck for cover when the going gets tough - as Nottingham Forest have found to their cost this season.'

'If foreign players come here to accept our money then they should accept the traditions of our game - as we would theirs if we went to play in their country.'

'We are lucky here at Scunthorpe to have Alex Calvo García, our Spanish recruit. He is probably the most English among the foreign imports, and he for one has certainly not come across here for the money! He has settled in completely, speaks the language fluently and only occasionally now resorts to something in Spanish when he gets annoyed with himself. I have an idea what he means but I am not absolutely sure.'

Alex has integrated. After explaining to his new manager that he was never a striker, Laws has put him in midfield. He works hard in the gym, as Kevin Keegan did, to build up his body for the harshness of English football. The team are swimming around promotion in his first season as a regular starter. He has scored good goals and, when he does, he goes to the stands to embrace or slap hands with the fans, unfailingly pursued by the referee, worried about a possible overflow of passion. The fans chant 'García, García, García'. He has never enjoyed football so much.

In 1999, Alex is twenty seven. It is unlikely that a 'Bill Shankly' will come knocking to take him to Liverpool, but he is making a living in his favourite game. He is enjoying his adventure, travelling around England, learning about its language and culture. He has good friends in the team and in the town. His room-mate is goalkeeper Tom Evans, a steady and agreeable type, a university student who has returned home after trying his luck at Crystal Palace.

Brian Laws has cleaned out the disenchanted veterans from the dressing room. New players have joined the team and it is now an optimistic group. Mark Lillis, the assistant coach, plans training routines that are new and fun.

The Spaniard also gets on well with the club physiotherapist, Nigel Adkins, who had previously managed Bangor City in the Welsh

League. He has had opportunities to go to other teams with more money and ambition but his wife is ill. Scunthorpe is a good place to live and to him family comes first.

There are good players and good people at Scunthorpe United. In 1999, they are aiming for promotion. Alex wears the number eleven shirt. 'La Real' did not need him and in Eibar he failed to establish himself, but he is a good football player.

Laws asks him to fulfil the basic functions of a midfielder: up and down the pitch for ninety minutes. He is in good shape and, although he was never coached by Shankly, he shares his view that football is a simple game. His motto is not to complicate things, do what you know, hold the lines, protect your defence, keep your concentration to clear the ball. And when the team goes on the attack, show that you have something called class.

Javier Expósito, the man who signed him for Real Sociedad, had observed that Alex held the ball without fear. The ball is not an eel at his feet. He shows his special qualities when space is squeezed. His touches can be clever and accurate, he makes quick decisions. He was born with an instinct to find empty spaces on a crowded pitch. He scores often with his head.

One day, Laws joked on the training ground that, if Alex scored a goal from outside the area, he would show his backside to the whole ground. Alex duly scored from outside the area and team prankster Sean McAuley immediately hugged him and signalled to Laws demanding fulfilment of his vow.

At the end of the season, the team misses out on the possibility of automatic promotion but will be in the play-offs. Their opponent is Swansea City.

Paul Wilson, the youth team coach, the man who got lost with Alex while taking him to his digs on his first night in Scunthorpe, and who had been the oldest debutante in English professional football, at 37 years and nine months, when the club were unable to field eleven regular players in the team, videos the journey to South Wales.

In the beginning of the film, players get onto the bus on the day before the game. They pick up the rest of the team in petrol stations or road junctions. And then they play cards, sleep or read newspapers.

At the hotel, next morning after breakfast, they spend time hanging around halls and corridors or playing pool. McAuley, the joker of the team, takes a taco as an imaginary microphone for interviews, followed by Wilson's camera. He asks striker Jamie Forrester: 'How does it feel to be so small?' To veteran Russ Wilcox: ' Has playing with these types of footballers shortened your career?' To Justin Walker and Lee Marshall: 'What can you say about the rumour that you are a cross-dresser?' And to every member of the team: 'Are you using this club as a stepping stone?'

When Alex pokes his head through the door of the snooker room, McAuley asks, 'What do you think of the game?' Alex responds: 'Very excited.' And McAuley turns to the camera and translates: 'That's ve-ry ex-ci-ted.' The stigma of Manuel from Ordizia lingers on.

Scunthorpe lose one goal to nil at the Vetch Field, in a game with kicks off at half past twelve in order to avoid brutalities fuelled by alcohol. The return leg is played on a spring time Wednesday evening at a full Glanford Park.

Players practice their rituals in a tense dressing room. One kicks a ball against the wall, another lies on the floor. There is pop or rap music. The anxious crowd can be heard outside.

'Brian Laws barmy army. Brian Laws barmy army.'

The masseuse, Gina, talks to the camera and speaks on camera to Gareth Sheldon, who came through the youth ranks, 'Get a good picture of this guy, because he will come off the bench and score the winning goal.'

Brian Laws gives instructions.

'Everyone, Justin, Alex, make sure that the final ball is a good one.'

The assistant coach, Mark Lillis, individually encourages the players. They go out to warm up. Lillis leaves the field and returns with the flag of Saint George that he sticks in the penalty area. The fans chant the name of England. Then Laws and Lillis warm up with the players. John Gayle, the giant striker that Laws has signed to trouble defences, shakes hands with all his team-mates.

They return to the dressing room, unleashing a flurry of swearing. Fucking and fuck, all possible ways are explored. Laws launches into his last haranguing.

'No matter what happens tonight we have had a great season. Do not ever forget it. A season is not a fucking game.'

The players shake hands incessantly. They all shout. Between the screaming someone says: 'We are fucking Englishmen and proud of it!'

Alex's Scunthorpe United, representative of a town in which football flourished through a society built on immigration, enter the field to beat the Welsh enemy under the invocation of English pride. Football as always, a carnival of identities, faiths and nations.

Within two minutes, the sides are level on aggregate after a goal from Andy Dawson. But Swansea defend well and also create danger. When Scunthorpe get back to the dressing room at half-time, Laws scolds his goalkeeper, Tim Clarke, who has replaced Evans in order to deal with crosses.

'Your sense of anticipation has been shit...'

Clarke tries to talk. Laws will not let him.

'No, no... You have to make a decision. You have to be on your toes and move. You have to do better. So far you've been hesitating and that could cost me. I've put you there for a reason. OK? So do it right.'

No goals are scored in the second half. Before the end of full time,

Laws sends on Sheldon. In the second minute of extra time, he scores. The jubilation is short lived as Swansea quickly reply. Victory is in the hands of the Welsh thanks to the away goal rule. But Sheldon scores again in the second half of extra time.

'Fucking wankers! Come on, boys! Fucking bastards!'

The celebrations in the Scunthorpe dressing room begin with swearing and insults to no one and anyone, while captain Chris Hope and John Gayle enter the opponents dressing room to salute the defeated.

Paul Wilson leaves the camera and hugs 'Ginger' Sheldon, the man of the moment, whom he has coached in the youth team.

'My boy, my boy.'

The stands chant their joy. The players go back to greet their supporters, climb the stairs to the directors box, the fans are on the pitch. Players, board and directors all sing 'There's only one Gareth Sheldon'. And then another song, an Irish ballad for teetotallers often sung by drunks, 'The Wild Rover'.

Alex Calvo García's journey in English football heads towards its next stop, a Wembley final.

When the Scunthorpe players reach Wembley Stadium, the gates are closed.

There is nervous joking and the usual malarkey of McAuley, posing for the camera while removing blackheads from a colleague. 'This is called male bonding', explains McAuley to the cinematographer, Paul Wilson.

Someone finally finds the right buzzer. The players are not allowed to walk on the pitch but the electronic scoreboard confirms their right to be there: 'Wembley welcomes Scunthorpe United'.

A bunch of fourth division players, some still young and keen enough to dream of fame and fortune, others aware that this is their chance of a great swansong, roam the contour of the hallowed turf.

Brian Laws then reveals a secret. He has asked the stadium staff to pump up the volume and inundate the ground with a familiar noise. The speakers blast the wild roar of fans into the empty stadium. The players from Scunthorpe hear the noise, they look at the naked shape of the stands, its slight and long inclination towards the roof, the red and blue seats.

Laws has already told them the story. Brian Clough warned the Forest players, who had reached a final, about the anxiety of footballers when they play at Wembley. Laws took notice and devised a plan to tame the nerves. Right at the start of the game, he was going to move back from the line of defence, offer himself to the goalkeeper, collect the ball, roll it back. Something simple, a million times done, feel the contact of the ball on the boot, make sure that he was capable of something minuscule and ordinary in the first minute.

But when the team came out of the tunnel, the fans saw the Garibaldi reds advancing towards the turf and let rip. Brian Laws wet himself. Not a lot, a brief pee in the white shorts of the Nottingham Forest holy uniform. And so he walked to the centre of the pitch to greet the guest of honour, Princess Diana of Wales.

Ten years later, the stadium is not hosting a big cup final. It is a rather more parochial affair, but he has asked his players to keep things simple in the opening minutes. And now, while walking around the perimeter of the pitch, the speakers emit the racket of the fans, so that Scunthorpe United footballers will not wet themselves when they enter the Wembley pitch.

English football's national stadium was built where it stands after a notorious failure to emulate the French. A Liberal MP and great patron of the railways, Edward Watkin, insisted, shortly after the Eiffel

Tower was built as the tallest building in the world, that London should have its own, but forty-six metres higher. Plans were approved, a surrounding park was designed, but the enterprise went bankrupt and almost everything was demolished. Watkin's dream became a base of four iron pillars and a structure less than fifty metres tall. The populace baptised the truncated junk as 'Watkin's stump'.

But, if the Eiffel tower was erected as the entrance arch for the Universal Exposition in Paris in 1889, Watkin's folly was destroyed to prepare the site for the Empire Exhibition in 1924. Costumes and crafts were on show: ostrich feathers and diamonds from South Africa, a life-size statue of the Prince of Wales on his horse made with butter from Canada, various Buddhas of Burmese marble, 'natives' doing a performance of their lives in Guyana huts, palaces of industry and engineering, doll houses of the Queen.

It was a financial disaster. Nothing appealed to the public as much as the Cup final between Bolton Wanderers and West Ham, the first to be held at the Empire Stadium. It would become known as the final of the white horse, Billy, the beautiful mount of a policeman, which managed to slowly shepherd the public from the pitch and back into the stands. The stadium was built in three hundred days by five thousand men with the capacity to accommodate one hundred and twenty-seven thousand spectators but, according to the newspapers, on that cup final day it was stretched to the seams to hold about two hundred thousand.

Since then, the stadium has been every May the venue for the final of the Football Association Cup, feeding the dream that a relative nobody in childish elation could climb the thirty nine steps leading to a box where princes awaited to present a silverware artifact. Wembley is the destination to which English players aim, the final stop in a game which tests the consistency of teams home and away over a long season but in The Cup present football in its primitive state, the challenge between two teams that meet at three o'clock in the afternoon on an English Saturday with everything at stake, winner takes all.

Wembley is also the place where the inventors of football discovered, one day in 1953, that the apprentices had surpassed them. England had lost against other national teams before – the first time against Spain at the Metropolitano stadium in Madrid, in 1929 – but the home defeat against Hungary dented their sense of superiority towards foreigners who had imitated their customs.

One of the defeated players of 1953, Alf Ramsey, was the manager of the England team that beat Germany at Wembley in the 1966 World Cup. It was the first football competition to reach spectators around the world through live television.

The twin towers, raised as the only stylish element in a stadium designed as a feat of engineering, were arquitectural pastiche, incongruous now among warehouses and factories of an industrial estate, in a landscape without trace of the exoticism seen at the Imperial Exhibition. But those towers were the Mecca of English football.

Before Scunthorpe knocked on closed Wembley doors, on the eve of the promotion finale to the Third Division, Brian Laws had prepared the team thoroughly. They had ten days to do so after eliminating Swansea in that wild night at Glanford Park. The first step was to go to Dublin to enjoy tribal drunkenness. Right after the match, Laws organised an expedition to spend a couple of days of inebriation. Beer, vodka and urine, as Brian Clough would have wished; the way that the intractable knot of brotherhood had been forever forged in English football. Laws initiative was popular with the directors of the club, who in 1992 had seen their manager, Bill Green, prepare the play-off final as 'just another game'. His idea was to not increase anxiety levels in his players. They lost on penalties. This time, the finalists run with a ball in some field at the hotel where they were staying, played golf, watched the Final of the FA Cup between Manchester United and Newcastle in a bar. Alex looked at himself in the reflection of an empty pint glass and struggles to believe it. In seven days he will be playing at Wembley and he is drunk. But Laws is content. The group has stayed together during the trip and he does not see anybody showing signs of fear.

While the team drinks, bonds and relieves itself in Dublin, the *Telegraph* asks its readers to write songs for the trip to London.

Eileen Granidge sends hers:

> *Bless 'em all, Bless 'em all*
> *We've fought long*
> *and hard for this call*
> *We've come here to Wembley*
> *Our steel town assembly*
> *So come on the Iron*
> *let's play ball.*
>
> *Bless 'em all, Bless 'em all*
> *The Iron won't lose*
> *We won't fall*
> *We're ready and dusted*
> *We are polished, not rusted*
> *So come on you Iron*
> *Show 'em all*
>
> *Bless 'em all, Bless 'em all*
> *We'll take oh, the cockneys and all*
> *We'll show our emotion*
> *When we win promotion*
> *And we'll cheer our lads*
> *Bless you all*

Chrissie Panter suggests her lyrics be accompanied by the music of 'Thank you for the music', a hit by 'Abba'.

> *Father said I was a fan*
> *Before I could walk*
> *He said I was cheering our team*
> *Before I could talk*
> *Me I've always wandered how did it start*
> *When did the Iron captured my heart*
> *Like a football team can - so I say*

> *Thank you for The Iron*
> *Our song I'm singing*
> *Thank you for the joy*
> *to Wembley bringing*

Karol Jury asks that her offering be sung along to the 'reggae' tune of 'Iron, Lion, Zion', by Bob Marley:

> We're the Iron
> like the Lion
> for Brian

Laws is the leader of the pack, but the *Telegraph* set aside space for the club's first foreign footballer, who came from the Basque forges to the Ironpolis of Scunthorpe and stayed.

'If you carry out a poll of supporters for the club most popular player, few would be surprised if the name at the top was Spanish. Alex Calvo García has impressed everyone during his virtually ever present run of the past two seasons. His skills so typically continental, his work-rate typically English.'

The team returns from Dublin. They study videos of their rivals, Leyton Orient, the first professional football club to tour Spain, in 1914. They were then known as Clapton Orient and their rivals were clubs from the Basque region. They had played in the First Division in the sixties. Their main shareholder is now a boxing promoter, their star player is Amara Simba, a former French international, doing his final rounds in professional football.

The Scunthorpe team analyse videos of their opponent, practice defence and attack routines, and on Friday morning they head south on the team bus. Their hotel is a redbrick Victorian mansion, with a classical pediment façade and over-elaborate patterned carpets. They awake there on the morning of the game. Standing naked, players appear at their windows, some mock female pantomime voices. Paul Wilson films it all. It is a sunny day. The weather forecast says that it is going to get warmer in the afternoon.

After an early lunch, the team meets for the penultimate instructions.

'You have played forty nine fucking games', Laws says. 'No one will remember you as losers. Winners are remembered. Today we can be winners. Come on.'

The team board the coach that will take them to the stadium. The impassive John Gayle, the only black man of the squad, has already played twice at Wembley. He greets the camera: 'Peace on Earth.'

When the bus arrives to Wembley and moves through the mass of fans, Alex gets goosebumps.

They have been lucky in the draw for the changing rooms. Superstition or statistics show that the occupants of the one with the England crest most often win. Both teams have a waiter to serve drinks, but Leyton Orient have to settle for a fresco depicting a samurai on the wall.

On the notice board there is a telegram from Kevin Keegan

sending his best wishes. Electronic dance music is blasting out. Gayle, as always, listens to his own music on his headphones.

When he enters the field to warm up, Alex looks into the stands to find his girlfriend, his parents and in-laws. At the last moment, there was a mistake with airports. Will anyone from home be at Wembley? He steps onto the turf. The bounce of the ball surprises him. A hard surface.

When they return to the locker room, Laws reminds the players about their positioning at dead ball situations and pronounces his final message.

'One fucking chance! Only fucking winners are remembered. Be a winner! Be a winner!'

John and Val Costello, who go to every game, are, of course, in Wembley. They helped Alex in his difficult early days as a footballing immigrant. John was a professor of Spanish and French whose concept of belonging to a community included lending a hand to this young man who had just arrived from Spain. They have shared adventures and misadventures of the team because they see it as sap nourishing a sense of identity, of locality, of common history. They have never wanted to be directors because they did not want to participate in boardroom politics or keeping secrets, feeling that their place was with ordinary fans. They always applaud the team at the end of every game, home and away, win or lose. And now they are enjoying a galactic experience.

They have travelled to London and their daughter, who works at a bank, presents them with a loving gift. Her company has a box at Wembley, where they invite guests to enjoy the big games. But when John and Val enter the box, they realise that it rises above an empty part of the huge stadium. It can seat eighty thousand but is today half full. There is waiter service but a glass window insulates them from the mob, and today of all days, the most joyful of all for followers of Scunthorpe United, John and Val Costello will watch the game silently floating above the humanoid passion of football in some kind of flying saucer for VIPs.

At the same time, Andy Lister and his friends, who stand together in the last row of the stands at Glanford Park, making more noise than anyone, fulfilling their duty, their place in battle, their impetus to give soul to their team and challenge rivals, are excited and exhausted.

Andy set off in the morning by bus from Scunthorpe and has already lost his voice:

> *She wore, she wore, she wore*
> *a scarlet claret ribbon.*
> *She wore a scarlet claret ribbon*
> *in the merry month of May,*
> *and when I asked her*
> *why she wore that ribbon,*
> *she said it's for United*
> *and we're off to Wembley, Wembley, Wembley.*
> *We are the famous Scun United*
> *and we're off to Wembley.*

He has sung until his throat is raw. But it is all worth it. Since that day, when he was twelve, when he first went to Glanford Park and heard the chants and screams, saw the painted blue faces of rival Cardiff City fans, the colours, sweat, blood and smell of football, he has only missed games while studying away from Scunthorpe. Since then, and for eleven years, home and away, he is often the one leading the choir in heartfelt stanzas:

> *With an S and a C,*
> *and the U, N, T.*
> *H and an O and an R, P, E.*
> *United!*

Andy, tireless in his chanting, goes wild at times but he is not a hooligan. He has never punched anyone. He works in a bank, has a girlfriend and enjoys following Brian Laws' barmy army. He knows that his team will never win the FA Cup, but he still wants to get out of the basement division. So with a hoarse voice he sings the hymns and ballads of the tribe, at last at Wembley. We are here, we have succeeded. He observes the mass of followers. All in claret and blue T-shirts, scarves, and many in jester hats bearing flags.

They mock the Cockneys of Orient, 'You must have come in a taxi.' And sing again: 'Wembley, Wembley, we are the famous Scunthorpe United and we've come to Wembley, Wembley, Wembley.'

At the same time, Ken Rounce turns on the radio at home. He is one of the oldest followers. He used to go to the Old Showground as a child and attended the Christian Sunday school, created by the club founders, the lawyer Symes and the secretary Allcock, a member of the Methodist Church in the high street now replaced by a supermarket.

Ken has seen the town and the club grow and shrink. His grandfather worked the land in Norfolk but his father was interested in machinery, so they moved to Scunthorpe and set up their own garage. He grew up in a town that for entertainment showed the silent films of Charlie Chaplin and had the football games at the Old Showground. And the 'Keenites' youth club would take them from time to time to watch Huddersfield Town or Sheffield Wednesday.

Then the war came. Ken Rounce landed in Normandy on D-Day with a mobile workshop. He saw more war in the Ardennes, in the Baltic and in Hamburg, arriving back in one piece. He found a job in the steelworks. He continues to go to Glanford Park for the buzz the game gives him, but now it is not like the old days, when football was played in a ground with just one stand, with hard leather balls and heavy boots, and there were fewer injuries.

And too many people go to the match just to drink.

Ken Rounce turns on the radio. He does not want the TV channel that broadcasts football at all hours. Nor does he want the discomfort of travelling to London and back. He lives a quiet life. Maybe this time the club will achieve the ever present ambition of promotion.

At the same time, Don Rowing, club secretary, is sitting in the director's box. He has managed the finances of the club for nearly two decades and knows the accounts by heart. Half of the revenue comes from league funds, from television rights and sales in the souvenir shop. The rest has to come from gate receipts and the trade on players. In the past twenty years, wages have risen more than seventy-five percent while attendance has fallen. The objective is to bring players from the youth team and that their salaries are no more than sixty percent of the expenditure, so that the cost of all the employees does not exceed three quarters of the budget. Thus the club will not be in danger.

As a child, Don followed rivals Doncaster Rovers, but this is professional football, he knows the accounts of all the clubs in the division. Rowing is the administrator who blends ambition with reality, allowing the fans to postpone their hopes until next season.

Every year he receives an invitation from the Football League to watch the play-off final but he has never taken it. This time he has come. On the night of the semi-final he had a fax ready with an order of t-shirts and scarves to suppliers. Everything has sold out. All the bus seats, all the tickets. In the stadium there are thirteen thousand people who have come from Scunthorpe, a quarter of its population. Grown men are laughing and crying. He feels proud to be at Wembley. And he tells himself: 'We are Scunthorpe United and we are here to do the business. We are going to win promotion.'

At the same time, Bob Steels is getting changed. He was a child when he first saw Scunthorpe United. The football writer in the *Telegraph* during Steel's childhood was Tom Taylor, father of former

England manager, Graham Taylor. The journalist and Kevin Keegan had a cabaret act to entertain guests at dinner parties. Keegan sat on Tom Taylor's knee, the future star of world football pretending to be a ventriloquist's puppet.

Steels has driven his car with his wife and two friends as passengers, along with the caravan of buses heading south. He also feels proud of the town. Scunthorpe is not a place that gives its residents many opportunities to puff their chests. And now they head to Wembley, pilgrims to the shrine of English football. Bob Steels, *Telegraph* reporter, wears a claret and blue shirt on the way to Wembley but, after lunch, he removes his club shirt and changes into his work clothes, shirt and jacket, to enter the press box in his uniform of impartial journalist.

At the same time, Jerry Mahony, who in the last twenty years has only missed three Scunthorpe matches, who is also the mascot bunny, whose body is punished by Wilson's Disease, sits down at the bottom of the main stand. In his bag is his bunny uniform and the big rabbit head. The club is now a large part of his life. He loves the club and he knows that in this love there is also madness. He runs errands, helps prepare the stadium before games, organises visits to schools and dresses as a rabbit to entertain children. And he also has to put up with the drunken stupidity of hostile fans, who throw projectiles at him. Both dreams and suffering are without charge.

Sometimes he resents the behaviour of players and their healthy bodies. They earn a lot of money and never ask for forgiveness after a horrible game to fans who work hard to pay for the ticket. Jerry has tried to fix charity events, or fund-raising schemes for the club, without any player showing an interest or lending a hand. Scunthorpe's injured mascot is sitting in the stands, still excited about the win over Swansea, dreaming of a victory that will allow him to walk the Wembley turf to celebrate. Life is fairer and for just one moment it is close to happiness.

At the same time, Alex Calvo García is hiding in the toilets to evade the ban on mobile phones in the changing room. He wants to check that his family is in the stadium.

At the same time, his mother Mari Carmen is amazed. Not far from her seat, only minutes after setting foot for the first time in England, she sees a man wearing a Scunthorpe United Football Club shirt and on its back her surname, 'García', is printed.

Before heading out to the centre circle, Alex walks the line formed by the team to shake hands with Brian Laws, who hugs him. Alex is grateful. He has never enjoyed the game so much. The hard tarmac at the Urdaneta school, the Altamira gravel annex, the grass pitch in Ordizia, 'la Real', Beasain, Eibar. But this is Wembley. The teams make the short walk to the centre of the field, the fans roar, flags are fluttering. This time there are no prince or princess waiting, because this is the final for the promotion place to the third division. The players greet minor dignitaries – the guest of honour is the commercial director of a savings bank which sponsors the competition – and the national anthem plays. God save our gracious Queen. Long live our noble Queen. God save the Queen. Send her victorious, happy and glorious. Long to reign over us. God save the Queen.

Alex does not sing. But he knows that football is a game that commences at three o'clock in the afternoon on an English Saturday.

Orient kick off with a familiar pattern. The forwards pass the ball back to a midfielder who hits it long to the line, where a winger or a full back runs. This primeval cry of attacking will almost always ends surrendering the ball. This time it goes out for a throw to Scunthorpe.

There is no time to get an early touch, something simple to calm the nerves. The first fifteen minutes are a raging asphyxiating battle all over the pitch to get the ball forward and prevent the player you are marking doing anything adventurous.

Harsley goes up the left and crosses. Hicks, an Orient defender, clears the ball, it drops just outside the area. Alex beats an opponent in the air and heads the ball forward, bouncing to the goalkeeper; but 'García' has marked his territory, a will to prevail.

Scunthorpe recover the ball from the goalkeeper's kick and attack again down the left, Orient intercepts and try to counter. Their advance is slow, seemingly simple passes force the receiver to halt his run. But Richards delivers a good ball into the Scunthorpe area. Watts gets in front of Logan and shoots wide.

The ball is whizzing around. No team is imposing its rhythm. Wilcox now heads clear, the ball comes to Forrester with his back to goal. He gives it back to Dawson on the wing, who sends it long and high to Gayle, who heads back to the left, where Forrester has joined the attack, but a defender clears into the stands. Direct, simple geometry, old English football.

Dawson takes the throw and gives it to Forrester close to the byline. He turns and attempts to cross near the corner flag. A defender blocks. Forrester takes the throw quickly. Sheldon receives the ball on the edge of the area, pursued by his marker. He controls the ball with his chest, brings it down to his feet. He swivels, looking to get down the wing, the defender covers that angle, Sheldon turns inside and has enough space to cross towards the penalty spot.

García attacks the corner of the six yard box to meet Sheldon's cross, flicking the ball with his head towards the far post. Goal.

A combination of control, pass and move suddenly accelerated by a visionary and the touch known in football as class, the ability to tame a sphere of air and leather with any part of the body and direct it exactly to where you want it to go.

Scunthorpe have scored. Alex Calvo García has scored.

At Wembley. A great goal. He runs, dodging Sheldon's embrace, then Forrester, he takes off his shirt and reveals a white t-shirt with a Basque flag. He embraces Wilcox. Put your shirt on. Put your shirt on. His team-mates are going wild around the goal scorer, but Wilcox is worried that the referee will caution the Spaniard for breaking the etiquette dictated by football rulers for celebrations. The referee speaks to Alex, who puts his arm round the referee. It is fine. He learned a long time ago that referees in England talk and joke during the game. They are not fussy or authoritarian. If you complain they tell you to fuck off, and keep running.

In the stands, club secretary, Don Rowing, is thrilled and surprised. He had no idea that the first foreigner ever signed by the club harboured such intense feelings about his country of origin.

Plenitude follows. The game of football has become strangely easy. The ball is looking for him. He gets it high and sends it with his first touch into the path of Gayle. Too strong. He intercepts an opponent's embryonic counter, sliding on the ground. He takes the ball, stands up and gives it short. Alex the Basque is for a few short minutes the master of Wembley. Scunthorpe are composed. It is a mysterious switch. Harmony is found. Eleven players immerse themselves in a ballet for men in shorts. Passing and running, daring and supporting, timing and power.

Orient go for long and high balls. Evans is confident. Brian Laws put him on the bench for the semi-final and replaced him with Clark, thinking that he would be more effective with corner kicks and crosses. Now Evans has to play at Wembley. He is a steady character, a maths student who ended up as a professional football goalkeeper, he is not taking any of this too seriously. To him, Wembley looks good on television, but it is an old stadium, and the final is not an occasion to wave to your family, you have to do your job just like any other day. He will do it very well indeed.

Scunthorpe combine again down the left and Forrester lifts the ball with his toe towards Dawson, who had continued his run and volleys to goal. The keeper Barrett regales his crowd with a flowery save. But the game has lost the vivacity of the opening minutes and although appearing heroic is in reality pessimistic. Balls are kicked afar hoping for some luck in a combinatorial series of leaps and rebounds. Nobody commands possession, no side sustains incisiveness.

Scunthorpe are looking dangerous again down the left with Andy Dawson, the boy who trained with the Nottingham Forest youth system- where 'the correct way of playing football was taught'- and is now trying to swim back up the great river of professional football after being sold to the modest Iron. Dawson, Forrester and García are creating problems for Orient on the left side of the pitch because they are able to anticipate and combine, pass the ball where they want, take a tenth of a second advantage in the suffocating intimacy of rival athletes in professional football.

Orient attack with high balls to a tall defence, who can see them coming through the hot air. Occasionally there is a fortunate bounce, the flash of a chance. Simba moves with intelligence but their attack is slow and without bite.

Alex has the ball again, he is cornered by his marker and the byline. He keeps it on his toe, takes it away from his body, then a touch with the inside of the foot and he slips away for a second in the narrow strip between the marker and the byline. Nothing. But Wembley applauds the goal scorer.

The first half ends with a goalmouth scramble and failed clearances in the Scunthorpe area. A brief moment of anguish before the walk to the dressing rooms. Alex's team has played the better football.

Tommy Taylor, manager of Orient, replaces a defender and a midfielder with two forwards at the break. Scunthorpe are pushed back. Its sporadic counter attacks are easily broken. There is more nervousness now, tackles are harder, fatigue perhaps. It is very hot.

In the sixtieth minute the Iron do not defend a throw in well enough. Maskell reaches the byline, cuts the ball back to Watts, whose shot is blocked by Evans on the floor. Calvo García and Orient's Simba collide in the area disputing the loose ball.

The danger has passed. Nigel Adkins, Scunthorpe physio, takes the field to treat Alex and distribute drinks. On normal days he gives players orange soda with glucose, but this time he gives them water. Little details. He could have gone to other clubs with more swagger, but here he is handing out holy water to thirsty players of Scunthorpe United. On a hot day it is water, not glucose, what the players need.

It looks like Orient will score. The Iron quickly lose possession of the ball. They have no composure. The left-footed Lockwood, in the red and white midfield, is hitting good balls to the flanks. The exhausted 'García' is replaced by Housham, Gayle by Stamp. Laws wants more mobility and energy. Orient are not taking their chances. Sighs, nerves, tick-tock.

With just four minutes to play, Simba again plays a good ball to Inglethorpe but Evans saves his shot. There is only time left for last minute drama, but this time at the other end. A solo run by Stamp, he shoots and Lind clears.

They do not score their second goal, but Scunthorpe United Football Club have won promotion. An early strike and stubborn resistance. Alex has scored the winning goal at Wembley. Coaches and substitutes run onto the pitch, hugging those who finished the game. Paul Wilson takes his video camera and starts filming. Justin Walker screams to the lens: 'You get it! You fucking cockney wankers! And I'm one of them!'

It is time for things to get silly. Jerry Mahony, wearing his mascot uniform, leaves his seat and enters the pitch. The Bunny joins the party. Someone embraces him, raises him with his arms and drops him. Mahony, the rabbit, crashes down hard on the holy grass of Wembley.

A radio journalist approaches the directors box and asks the club chairman, Keith Wagstaff, about the game and how he feels. He is about to say something, but breaks down in tears.

He has been the chief executive of a public company, but this is something different. He was a young footballer with Lysaghts, saw Scunthorpe when he was ten and was hooked. Being the chairman of the club is enjoyable, because a football club is an organisation that now and then enjoys success and everybody wants to be part of something successful. He believes that a football club is a unique company. Yes, there are budgetary controls and commercial decisions, but the camaraderie of the players in a football team does not exist in any other. It is a distinct spirit that spreads to all its followers. The closing of a contract worth ten million pounds never moved him as Alex's goal and the fulfilment of the dream of promotion. So Keith Wagstaff cries.

Then he recovers to speak to the reporter, 'Just look at that crowd. I've never seen anything like it in my life. I'm so proud. I'm delighted for the people of Scunthorpe.'

Brian Laws' barmy army is today the ideal community of winners. They form a procession going up to the Royal box to repeat what Bobby Moore did in 1966. The same ritual seen every May in the FA Cup final. The captain, the austere and classy defender Chris Hope, raises the cup. The claret and blue tide roars, the players receive their medals, go down the steps, walk around the pitch waving to their fans, posing for pictures with wigs, scarves, hats, between hugs and laughter behind the sponsors banner.

Russ Wilcox leaves the group and walks to an area of the pitch where he can see his father, somewhere in the higher tiers. Wilcox is thirty five years old. There are few winters left for him playing professional football. It all started when he was a boy, going hand in hand with his father to see Doncaster Rovers. Later came the training, the contracts, the dream of once and for all getting out of the Fourth Division. At Northampton he won promotion. Nine years later, he did it again with Preston. Since then, no more promotions. He had never been to Wembley. And now, when his journey through the regions of lower league football is coming to an end, away from everyone, he searches for his father. Up there in the stands, experiencing his own countdown, a terminal illness that is eroding him.

The players retire to their changing room. Has anyone in the world given so much happiness through their work as the Scunthorpe players today?

Paul Wilson regrets that he was not given the chance to play earlier in the Football League. He was good enough but managers demanded exorbitant fees when other clubs wanted to sign him. He got a reputation for having too much movement in the ankle after failing a medical at the beginning of his career, but played for 15 years in the Conference, amazing colleagues with his running. Later, he went to play in Australia, only to return because family life demanded it. He feels that he was led, kidded, if only those people had not taken it away from him. One thing he learned then was to always tell the truth to a youngster in his charge.

He was Alex's chauffeur in the early days of bewilderment in England. He helped him in the first months to train in the mornings while the others had afternoon sessions, firmly believing that this is a game in which players must be fit. He has been part of the trip and filmed it all. And now he is the only one left on the pitch, still dreaming of what might have been, the one carrying the cup home.

Jerry Mahony is going through a comical entanglement. A steward is preventing him returning to the stands, where he has left his bag and clothes. He is dressed up as a rabbit, trying to convince the steward that he is an honest man, striving to make himself understood with his voice distorted by Wilson's Disease. The steward finally allows him to return to his seat. Jerry will not have to travel back to Scunthorpe, on a hot day, wearing his bunny outfit.

In the changing room, the players throw Laws into the bath, followed by Gina, the masseuse.

The journalists who are waiting outside ask Alex how he feels: 'I love the people of Scunthorpe. They have made me happy since the day I came to the club. I think I now have made them very happy too- so perhaps now that makes us even.'

Players' families tell each other to meet at the welcome party for the victors at Glanford Park. The long road home.

When players and officials get on the bus, they realise that no one had anticipated a victory celebration. Scunthorpe do not spend in champagne, Wembley or not. The cautious passion of a club created by Methodists is now a bad joke. So the coach stops when a supermarket is spotted and chairman Wagstaff and vice chairman Garton return from their expedition with cans of beer and pork pies. And the occupants of the bus sing all the way home.

Normality is quickly restored. Some players get off at Nottingham, others at the petrol station where they left their car on route the day before. The bus arrives at Glanford Park just after midnight, where they are met by a handful of fans and family.

There is an open top bus tour of the town planned but no official reception. People at the club complain that the council is not interested in football, even though the suspect name of the town is broadcast each week all around the country when the BBC voices, neat and perpetual, read the football results on a Saturday afternoon. There is no more than a brief flurry of excitement at Glanford Park, a family affair. Alex's mother, who many years ago crossed the road that separates Altamira from the rest of Ordicia with baby Alex in her arms and her husband under arrest, still marvels at how the fans are chanting again her surname: 'García! García!' The man from Radio Humberside climbs to the top of a car and reproduces word by word his commentary on air of 'García' goal.

The *Telegraph* headline reads: 'Glory boys'. And publishes letters from fans. They complain about the indifference of the council regarding an event which has caused such a stir in the town. Someone writes that the Council should honour the imported goal scorer of Wembley by naming a street after him. García Way.

In *When Saturday Comes*, a magazine that inspired a new style of football writing, stepping aside from the aseptic tone of newspaper journalism and publishing the copy of biased fans, 'Harry' writes 'Living next to Alex'.

'There has been a dangerous outbreak of optimism around both club and town. Supporters believe the club can survive in the Third Division and possibly go further, and the much-mulled-over shopping centre redevelopment has finally been given the green light in a devil-may-care moment of brazen progressiveness. Doubtless the councillor who signed the dotted line is now locked in his office, mopping his brow in a fevered burst of 'Dear God, what I have done?' Because he knows that the bubble may burst some time over the next year and that we may well find ourselves once again with our heads bowed to the ground. But we lived off a play off final defeat for almost seven years and we'll live off this victory for many more. We are sure to be cold and miserable and grey grey grey again one day, but we will always be able to remember a modest little Spaniard running his socks off at Wembley and nodding the town into the present.'

Days later, Gayle is released. Forrester signs for Utrecht. Eyre for Hull. Lillis leaves to take charge of Halifax Town. Andy Dawson, the left back who played so well at Wembley, talks with people about the game and the euphoria, 'but you do not have those emotions anymore and you can never feel them again.'

The Scunthorpe United board are facing their eternal dilemma. Should they spend money to buy a few good players, risking bankruptcy if they fail to stay up? The club opts for economical survival.

Alex gets injured in the winter. The television company which had bought the rights to broadcast the matches in the lower divisions reneged on their contract. Some clubs struggled to keep their creditors at bay. Scunthorpe survived. Alex recovered from his injury. When he came back, he ran and showed touches of class. Scunthorpe were relegated. He attracted offers from other clubs but preferred to stay in the suburbs of the industrial garden town, next to the steelworks, in the almost forgotten region of North Lincolnshire. Leire was happy there as well. They had a nice house. And a second child was on the way.

At the beginning of the 2003/04 season, Alex announced that it would be his last. He was returning home. The club gave him his farewell in a match between the veterans of the 1999 final and a team with Spanish players based in England: Roberto Martínez, pioneer at Wigan, Gaizka Mendieta of Middlesbrough, Zigor Aranalde of Walsall. Jordi Cruyff, who had left Manchester United, flew from Vitoria, where he was playing for Alavés.

Alex's last season had been the worst for Scunthorpe in recent years. Brian Laws was restored as manager a few days after his dismissal. The club kept its promise, everything could be better next season.

8 January, 2005, is wet and blustery. The streets of Carlisle are flooded, the M62 motorway is closed in parts and travelling by car is only recommended to those who really must.

Six thousand Scunthorpe fans really have to travel south, where Roman Abramovich's Chelsea await in the third round of the FA Cup. Brian Laws' barmy army had been top of the fourth division at the beginning of the season but are now second. Alex, Leire and the children left in the summer.

The drama and discomfort of the previous season has faded like a bad storm, clearing the air. The team is in an automatic promotion place and they have been drawn against one the most fashionable clubs in the world, with a squad bought by a Russian tycoon and managed by a Portuguese coach.

The match at Stamford Bridge will leave three hundred thousand pounds in the bank for the visitors. Scunthorpe's budget sorted for the next two or three seasons.

In the old stadium of Fulham Road, supporters came through turnstiles and stood in the stands. The new stadium is the result of a large development of the site. Twenty-first century Chelsea Village is a sports entertainment complex, including hotels and conference centre facilities. Stewards now kindly indicate fans to their seats. Tickets cost fifty pounds. There are corporate boxes, carpeted hallways, heating radiators hang from the upper terrace roof to make the winters less unpleasant, toilets have porcelain sinks, marble urinals and hot air dryers.

'United! United!'

The Daily Mail describes the match as a contest between paupers and princes and it publishes a table comparing two possible starting line-ups and their cost. Chelsea's eleven is about 160 million pounds. Scunthorpe's is nil, all recruited at the end of their contracts with other clubs.

But there are in sports recurrent themes drawn from the biblical tale of David and Goliath. For every Piggott or Telemaque enduring discrimination towards the 'negro', a Constantine has always risen in the fields. For every prediction based in history or science, a team like Munster will beat one day a team like the All Blacks. Because there is always among the 'domestiques', carrying food, drinks and messages to leaders of their team, one who is planning to break away from the 'peloton' and reach the finishing line after an insane and lonely ride, and then be taken exhausted to a podium to be kissed by two misses, among flowers and stridently coloured maillots.

It happens in the sixth minute on this wet and windy day, watched by forty thousand spectators at Stamford Bridge. Matt Sparrow gets the ball to Paul Hayes, who turns in the area, leaves the Russian Alexei Smertin behind and sweeps the ball into the net past Italian Carlo Cudicini, who until that moment had been busy popping claret and blue balloons brought by the festive Scunthorpe fans.

The large screen of the stadium repeats the goal in slow motion, so that customers can enjoy the full Chelsea football show.

'Who are you? Who are you?', jest the choir from North Lincolnshire. And even in the corporate seats, where football is watched with the cool dignity of theatre spectators, two or three are onto their feet, who are you? who are you?, clapping and cheering and getting carried away.

'Stand up if you love Scunthorpe! Stand up if you love Scunthorpe!'

Are they paid extras among the crowd to give others a football experience as if this was a theme park?

The dream ends in the twenty-fifth minute. The Icelander Eidur Gudjohnsen and the Ivorian Didier Drogba create enough trouble around the Scunthorpe defence for a hurried clearance to fall on the Serbian Mateja Kezman's path, who volleys into the net.

Shortly after the start of the second half, just after the palate of the nouveau riche of football has been murdered with a distressing mix of biscuits and Pinot Noir on their reserved tables at half time, Drogba, the most expensive foreign player in English football history at the time of his signing, goes down the left again and sends a deadly cross. Andy Crosby deflects into his own net.

And then, before Scunthorpe throw everything at Chelsea and have three good chances to score; before Cleveland Taylor, detached and incisive as ever, hits the post with a header; before the third Chelsea goal is scored and Goliath smashing of David restores reality; before all of this, Stamford Bridge hears for the first time, on this wet and windy day, the chant for all journeys, in victory or defeat.

'Scunthorpe till I die, I'm Scunthorpe till I die.'

Saturday 11 August, 2007, is a sunny day. The train crosses London to The Valley. In 1919, Charlton fans wanted something better for their team and they dug an old chalk quarry to create a pitch. They piled the debris on the sides and an artificial valley was made to watch football games.

In Waterloo East station, a middle-aged man and two teenagers with United shirts board the train. In the seats opposite, two heavily built men, who are talking loudly, note their arrival with malicious smiles, mocking the visitors from the north.

Charlton was a well run club, which had kept the same manager, Alan Curbishley, for fifteen years. He left in 2006 and the board then dared to spend more to keep them in the world's richest league. But Charlton had three managers that season and were relegated.

Walking to the ground, two young men are wearing Real Sociedad shirts, last year's kit. After forty years in the Spanish first division, Alex's team has been relegated. A transit from identity football to consumerism of coaches and players, and ruin.

It is the first game of the season. Scunthorpe is in the second division, now renamed The Championship.

It has been three years since Alex returned home. His last season was the worst in recent years. After he left, Brian Laws took the team to promotion again. They managed to avoid relegation with some good signings, paid with money from the game in Chelsea. In November 2006, when the Iron were in a position to go up again, Laws was offered the manager's job at Sheffield Wednesday and Scunthorpe let him go.

The board handed the reins to Nigel Adkins, who had devoted many hours to helping Alex get through injuries. He was the bright professional who had offers from other clubs but stayed in Scunthorpe as physio and goalkeeping coach while his wife was ill. Adkins' Scunthorpe finished top of the table. The Iron are now in the second division for the first time in forty odd years.

While the fans are crowding around the visitors turnstiles, a group sings, 'Tu-turu-turu-turu-tu'. A chorus responds: 'Tu-turu-turu-turu-tu'. Prisoners in a concentration camp humming the secret code of a plan to escape to victory.

The fans pass through a narrow passage to the stands, where almost all the doormen and stewards are black. Scunthorpe fans, white. Anxious looks from the stewards, from the black girl in the hut serving beer, tea, cakes. A steward says: 'You can tell they aren't from London or Birmingham, they're from the countryside.'

From the iron fields.

The article on the visiting team in the match day programme begins with this sentence: 'They come from the relatively deserted wasteland of Lincolnshire football …' A writer patting heads of the unknown.

Adkins comes out in his shorts and football boots to run the warm-up drills, and the supporters sing the latest chant to celebrate his success. Music by Verdi, 'La Donna è Mobile'.

'Who needs Mourinho? Who needs Mourinho? We've got our physio! We've got our physio!'

But the songs are drowned by the PA, which bombards an anthem of U2 for sunny afternoons. And then the punk existentialism of The Clash at the end of the Cold War.

Adkins gives individual instructions to his players. They embrace and joke with him. There is happiness in this Scunthorpe team, on this beautiful day.

The PA announces that it is forbidden to watch the game standing. But the fans are already on their feet while on the pitch Charlton's chairman is signing the contracts of his two new players. The first, a Frenchman, Thierry Racon, is greeted by the Scunthorpe fans.

'Who are you? Who are you?'

And now a young Chinese player, Zhen Zhi, who was wanted by two big clubs but has chosen to return to his old club. A touching story?

'Who are you? Who are you?'

As the match begins, the visitors ghetto is invaded by the last wave of supporters, rushing after finishing their last pints. They are an unruly mess, ignoring all access protocol, jumping over the rails to find their seats, arms raised, hands clapping.

'We are Scunthorpe! We are Scunthorpe!'

The tattooed, the ugly, the ruddy faced, the fat. A large woman with ample breasts also jumps the fence. A fifty year old man, with eyes illuminated by alcohol, loses his balance and falls onto a fan, who helps the drunk to move up. We are Scunthorpe! We are Scunthorpe! The brotherly troops support each other. Stewards and police try to impose order. But only the slow are detained, indignant that someone in a yellow jacket would want to hinder the fraternity of the mob, forcing them to return the way they came and enter the stands by the ever so boring back door.

Football is a game that commences at three o'clock in the afternoon on an English Saturday.

'We are Scunthorpe! We are Scunthorpe!' The team has the ball, it moves and passes well, looking for flaws in the rivals' defence, but it is a mirage. Soon possession is lost, Charlton are allowed to combine. If they had more speed, more inventiveness, more class with the last touch, they would have broken this classic defence. Giants with stiff backs, great for the team pictures and for composing a great body shape to kick the ball thirty metres away, where something may happen. But nothing happens.

The same pattern in the second half as Scunthorpe fail to maintain the ball. Charlton score. And now that the home fans are noisy the away support counter-attacs: 'You only sing when you're winning, sing when you're winning!'

Standing and clapping now, yes, but where are the brave who travelled to York on that freezing night? Where the utterly mad who did not flinch at the gales or the desolation of that match in Swansea? Their unyielding loyalty must live submerged in this crowd.

A corner for The Iron. Charlton's defence desert their cause and Izzy Iriekpen heads into the net.

'Na-na, na-na! Na-na-na-na! Scunthorpe!'

And when the team reassembles, settles and plays their rich London counterparts as equals, the song of unconditional faithfulness is heard.

'Scunthorpe till I die. I'm Scunthorpe till I die. I know I am. I'm sure I am. I'm Scunthorpe till I die'.

The first game in the second division ends in a draw and a line of buses wait outside the ground to take their human cargo.

It is a beautiful warm evening. God has been dead for a time. The nation still sings to the dream of a new Jerusalem, but feels unease and is again at war. Of the utopia of the cooperative garden town, only the private cultivation of roses has survived. But the communal dream of football has made the travelling fans happy on their way home.

EPILOGUE

Scunthorpe went to the new Wembley stadium in 2009 to beat Millwall in the play-off of League One. Nigel Adkins kept the team in the Championship and moved to Southampton early in the 2010/11 season.

After spells with Sheffield Wednesday and Burnley, Brian Laws returned to Scunthorpe for a third time in October 2012. He could not avoid relegation to League Two and lost his job early in the next season, after a draw at Blundell Park and a home defeat against local rivals, Grimsby Town, in the FA Cup.

After the retirement of chairman Steve Wharton, the new owner of the club, Peter Swann, had set a target for United to become a club at the top half in League One.

Brian Laws's assistant, Russ Wilcox, replaced him and established a record in the Football League with an unbeaten run of 28 matches. His team finally lost 2-0 at Exeter in April of 2014. But a deluge did not damp celebrations, as other results meant that The Iron was back in League One.

After the final whistle, Wilcox went to salute the away supporters at St. James, stopping for a few seconds under the downpour to point his fingers to the skies, as he had done fifteen years before looking for his father seat, high in the Wembley terraces.

In 2009 Real Sociedad commemorated its centenary by earning promotion to Primera División after three years in Segunda, from which Eibar had been relegated in 2006. The small town club fluctuated between the lower divisions until 2014 when, for the first time in its history, they won promotion to the top league of Spanish football.

Eibar was run with the same principles that Alex Calvo García knew when he played for the club before leaving for Scunthorpe. With an average gate of three thousand they had no debts, but were forced by the directors of La Liga to raise more than one million pounds of capital as a requisite to be part of the indebted elite of Spanish football. They raised the money with a public appeal to supporters and sympathisers, while keeping a limit of 2% of their shareholdings in the hands of any one individual.

In October of 2015 Scunthorpe was hit by the announcement that nine hundred jobs could be lost at the steelworks. There is too much steel in the world markets and the people of the North Lincolnshire town wondered about their future if their century-old industry was made redundant by forces beyond their control.

The owner of Scunthorpe United, Peter Swann, laid out plans to build a new stadium, a mile from Glanford Park, in a stretch of land that the council had marked as a development area, Lincolnshire Lakes, on the other side of the M181.

A stadium for ten thousand spectators was part of a project to build amenities, a business park, artificial lakes and new houses to meet the expected population growth in the area, where the government wants to create in the Humber the largest deep water port in Britain, catering to the needs of new industries of renewable energy.

After their return, Alex and Leire created a business in Beasain, where they live with their children. He had obtained a diploma from the Open University and their company, Innovatek, offered IT services to local businesses. The homecoming was a frantic time but still he felt that he was an English footballer.

He could not speak Spanish on a pitch.

'When you play football, the more you talk the more you are involved and I had been speaking English daily for eight years in training and matches. Here I was playing a seven-a-side game with friends and could not talk in Spanish, it was weird. I felt a bit embarrassed about what others would think of me but the jargon of English football came to my mouth naturally: hold it, squeeze, man on, handball... But with the passing of time things have changed and now I only swear in English when playing a game.'

In 2008, his team, Zuma GH, won the Spanish and European championship of seven-a-side football. Luis Garmendia was another player on that team. He had been on trial in Scunthorpe a few days before the arrival of Alex.

Reminders of his travels in English football were frequent. Tomás García de la Plaza, who had reported on the first Spaniards in English football when he worked in London, made a documentary on Alex's farewell to Scunthorpe. It was broadcast by a television channel in Madrid.

Another journalist, Luis Villarejo, was moved by the film and wrote about Calvo García in 'Made in Spain', included in a collection of articles, 'La Futbolería', where various authors write about different football adventures.

Goierri Telebista, a television channel covering an area that includes Ordizia and Beasain, made a documentary on their English returnee and Leire and Alex were constantly approached by neighbours asking about their experience.

They were one day walking by San Sebastián bay and were approached by two foreign-looking guys. 'Are you Alex?' asked one of them. He had a poster of him in his bedroom growing up in Scunthorpe. His friend was from Leeds but a supporter of The Iron. They were on a year trip around the world and stopping in San Sebastián they had seen a familiar flag a few minutes before. That flag was the one worn by

Alex in Wembley under his club shirt. This must be the Basque Country, one said. Alex must have come from here. And then they see Alex walking towards them with his wife and kids.

Calvo García goes sometimes to watch Real Sociedad. A friend gives him his season ticket when he cannot attend. And who sits in front of him? Phil Ball, a Grimsby Town supporter living with his family in San Sebastián, author of a great chronicle on Spanish football, 'Morbo', a writer who observes of course players and tactics but widening the lens to capture characters among the crowd, the history and culture that sustains such a popular game.

Gaby Ruiz, erudite and cool commentator of international football for television channel Canal Plus, travelled to Scunthorpe to make a documentary that reached a wide Spanish public. It was received with praise for the makers of the film and for its protagonist, 'Alex Calvo García, mito del Scunthorpe'.

Time may dilute emotion but when the mother of Alex, Mari Camen, feels low she orders her brain to wander back to Wembley for things to look brighter. The father, José Miguel Calvo, still displays a sticker of Wembley stadium on his car.

John and Val Costello go to every match of The Iron, home and away. They took Leire in their car. In their return trip from one of those expeditions, winter cold chastened the spirits. But John did not put the heating on. Val interceded. 'Do you feel cold?', she asked Leire, travelling in the back. But John explained that switching on the air conditioning was against his principles because a hot car can cause somnolence to the driver. 'The driver has to feel comfortable', he pronounced.

Alex is the opposite of John. He is very keen on feeling warm when he is driving. And when Leire attempts to turn off the heating, she laughs when Alex replicates in English what they have rehearsed many times remembering their friends: 'The driver has to feel comfortable.'

Viola Rowbottom, friendly host of Alex in his hardest days as the mute player of Scunthorpe United, had cooked a Christmas turkey for hours. Alex and Leire were shocked when Viola's husband, John, then drowned the dish with brown sauce. Such a gastronomic sacrilege in the eyes of the foreigners was told to their families back home as palpable proof of the idiosyncrasies of the English. The mother of Leire, Dori, turned Rowbottom to her own Spanish version, 'roboto', and since then, when someone pours an unlikely sauce on a meal, the family accuses the perpetrator of doing 'a roboto'.

In the early summer of 2015, Alex and Leire speak with great affection about their time in Scunthorpe, after lunch at a cider house in the hills surrounding Beasain and Ordizia.

'We were the two of us on our own. We had a profound relationship with our friends, they were somehow our family. We used to talk after dinner until the early hours about everything. We became adults there. And when we came back we felt clean. It was a tense political moment in the Basque Country and people argued frequently. People used to tell us that we spoke softly, like the English. Our minds were more open than before to different views. And we kept eating food that we tasted there for the first time, like Chinese meals or noodles. We drink tea.'

On his last day in Glanford Park, Alex Calvo García sat alone on the terrace after collecting all his stuff.

'I reflected about what I had lived there, about my relationship with the supporters. They respected me, they loved me. I would score a goal and three thousand people would go mad. People approached me in the supermarket to ask for an autograph. I was invited to go to hospitals and give presents to children. Nobody around me has had or will have that experience. Nobody is going to understand it. When I went back to Scunthorpe I felt deeply moved driving through the town. This had been our life and it wasn't any more.'

Alex sees now his experience as 'the legend' of Scunthorpe United as a distant past.

'I am not stuck in that time. I say to people that half of my heart is English and I say it with pride. I see it now as a bubble or a dream. I would not change my experience for Leo Messi's. I do not know what it means for him but the effect on me runs deep. I have read about footballers falling into depression when they retire, but I was very aware of how extraordinary it was. I enjoyed it so much. I look back at it with affection, of course, but it came to an end.'

The goal in Wembley was for Alex a culmination of everything that they had lived: the trip with Leire in the back of a van from Manchester airport to their new home in Scunthorpe, the hard times at the beginning and his success as a player in the team, their friendships, the birth of their children...

Now he rarely watches professional football.

'I follow the news on Scunthorpe and the English leagues on the BBC but I do not spend an entire afternoon watching football, except when it is a special match, like a cup final. If there is a match on the television screen when I am in a bar I may watch it but I'd rather be in a game of children. Spanish football bores me. There are things that remain with me. I detest players diving and faking injury, rolling on the pitch, referees intervening all the time. English football seems to me nobler, more real; it offers more in a game with more contact.'

Something else has happened to the legend of Scunthorpe United.

'I had said many times to Leire that I would never feel again the exhilaration of a goal but I have been surprised by the experience of coaching the 13 year-old team of Beasain. We are trying to inculcate basic concepts because many teams make shortcuts to score more goals. And when I see my team execute in a match something that we have taught them, something simple, like play the ball to the wing, run there to unbalance the rival in a two to one, I have felt the complete satisfaction that a footballer feels scoring a goal.'

'I tell you a story. There is a boy from Equatorial Guinea living in the town. His parents died in prison and his aunt brought him here. I met him in the gym and we used to talk, a very nice guy. One day he came to the gym saying that they needed one player for a seven-a-side game. And the day after he came laughing. He put me on the rival team and we trashed them, and all his mates had told him that he was an idiot because I had been a professional player in England, what he did not know. After all the hardships that he has suffered, he is a joyful guy, we like him a lot, he comes to our office to say hello and talk.'

'One day he was sitting on the ground with his tablet outside the workshop where he is employed and a truck ran over his legs. Doctors had to amputate one. But they were able to fit him with a prosthetic leg and came to the office happy to show us how good it was. So I asked him a favour. Would he speak to my team of 13-year-olds before our next match about falling and getting up again? And he did. I said to the kids that there would not be tactical talk, just Cristian speaking to them. I left the dressing room. They told me later that he was nervous at the start and that at one point he abandoned the notes that he had written and spoke to the kids about his life. There was plenty of crying. The boys played absolutely great and every goal-scorer ran to Cristian to dedicate his goal to him. How can you compare that with watching the final of the King's Cup?'

Alex with his wife Leire and their sons
Aidan (left) and Iakes (right) pictured outside their
home village of Beasain in June 2016.
In the background is Txindoki.

ACKNOWLEDGMENTS

Alex, Leire and their two sons, Aidan and Iakes, made me feel welcome at their home. They trusted me with their story and along the way we became good friends.

I am very grateful to the people of Scunthorpe who gave me their time and told me their own stories about Alex, Scunthorpe United Football Club and their town. Among them Nigel Adkins, Peter Beagrie, John and Val Costello, Andy Dawson, Vic Duke, Tom Evans, the late Rex Garton, Brian Laws, Andy Lister and his friends, Paul Longdon, Jerry Mahony, the late Ken Rounce, John and Viola Rowbottom, Don Rowing, John Staff, Keith and Nichola Wagstaff, Alan Webster, Russ Wilcox, the reverend Alan Wright, and Jack, Kate, Margaret, Paul...

Paul Wilson not only gave me his recollections, he gave me a disc with his film too, a wonderful present. Bob Steels at the *Evening Telegraph* and archivist Linda Roberts helped with my research beyond what is expected between colleagues. Martin and Rachel McLoughlin kindly sang and wrote down the chants of supporters for 'Iñigo from Barcelona' to finally understand them.

In San Sebastián and Ordizia I received generous help from Tomás Bosque, José Miguel Calvo and Mari Carmen García, Alfredo del Castillo, Javier Expósito and Iñaki Ibáñez. Jesús María Lariz searched his archives to guide me on the history of Ordizia and its football club.

Alberto Etxaluze, Patxi Mutiloa and José Antonio Rementería shared with me their knowledge of Sociedad Deportiva Eibar. The origin of this book goes back to the day when Tomás García de la Plaza, working then as a journalist in London, told me about a Basque guy who was playing for Scunthorpe United. The staff at the public libraries in Beasain, San Sebastián, Scunthorpe and Twickenham helped me find what I was looking for.

My dear friend, the late Stephen Hayward, was never interested in 'il calcio' but pointed to me in the direction of books, references, publishers... with customary erudition and good humour.

Matthew Kennington, an Iron supporter living in Madrid, bore the burden of an English translation as a labour of love. Peter Maguire and John Bew read an early draft and their words of encouragement were received with relief and delight.

With Walter Oppenheimer, Peter Maguire, Richard Curd and Andrew Morgan – and cameo roles by Paul Bew (Baron Bew of Donegore), Rafael Ramos, Patricia Tubella, Michael Byrne, John Bew and Martyn Frampton- I have watched matches of 'la Real', Barcelona, Seville, Jerez, Real Madrid, Valencia, Eibar, Getafe, Europa, Coria, Sanluqueño, Barakaldo, Mestalla, Huracán... guided on our trips to Spain by a demented question: What could be better right now than watching another game of football?

I would like to record my thanks to Toby Eady and the Ted Lewis Estate for granting permission to use the extract from Get Carter quoted on page 90. Thank you to the Dylan Thomas Estate for allowing us the quote from Under Milk Wood on page 5.

I have been fortunate in having James Corbett and Simon Hughes, at deCoubertin Books, as editors and publishers.

BIBLIOGRAPHY

Further to the books mentioned in the story, I am indebted to the authors of the following works.

Association Football and English Society, 1863-1915,
Tony Mason, HARVESTER PRESS, 1980.

The People's Game, **J.Walvin**,
TRAFALGAR SQUARE PUBLISHING, 1995.

The Football World, A contemporary social history,
Stephen Wagg, BRIGHTON HARVESTER PRESS, 1984.

Beastly Fury. The Strange Birth of British Football,
Richard Sanders, BANTAM PRESS, 2009.

Beyond A Boundary, **C.L.R.James**,
YELLOW JERSEY PRESS, 2005.

Football: A sociology of the Global Game,
Richard Giulianotti, CAMBRIDGE: POLITY PRESS, 1999.

The Code War, English football under the historical spotlight,
Graham Williams, YORE PUBLICATIONS, 1994.

The History and Antiquities of the Scunthorpe and Frodigham District,
Harold E. Dudley and George R. Walshaw, 1931.

An Industrial Island, A History of Scunthorpe.
Edited by **M. Elizabeth Armstrong,** 1981.

An Anglican-Methodist Covenant,
METHODIST PUBLISHING HOUSE, 2001.

The Professor, ARSÈNE WENGER at Arsenal,
Myles Palmer, VIRGIN, 2002.

The Great Transformation, The Political and Economic Origins of Our Time,
Karl Polanyi, BEACON PRESS, 1957.

Intelligence, Destiny and Education, The ideological roots of intelligence testing,
John White, ROUTLEDGE, 2006.

Urdaneta en su tiempo, **José Ramón De Miguel Bosch,**
SOCIEDAD DE OCEANOGRAFÍA DE GUIPÚZCOA, 2002.

La nao ballenera vasca del siglo XVI, **Miguel Laburu,**
PUBLICACIONES DE LA CAJA DE AHORROS MUNICIPAL,
DONOSTIA-SAN SEBASTIÁN, 1989.
OBRAS DE SAN IGNACIO DE LOYOLA,
BIBLIOTECA DE AUTORES CRISTIANOS, 1997.

Ignacio de Loyola, solo y a pie, **José Ignacio Tellechea Idígoras,**
EDICIONES SÍGUEME, 2000.

Villafranca de Guipúzcoa, Monografía histórica,
Carmelo Etxegarai y Serapio Múgica,
AYUNTAMIENTO DE ORDIZIA, 1983.

Santa Ana, Ordizia 2004, ORDIZIAKO UDALA, 2004.

Sociedad Deportiva Beasain, de ayer a hoy,
Miren Barandiarain Contreras, BEASAINGO PAPERAK, 2005.

Sport y autoritarismos: la utilización del deporte por el comunismo y el fascismo, **Teresa González Aja**, ALIANZA EDITORIAL, 2002.

Get Carter, **Ted Lewis**, ALLISON AND BUSBY CLASSICS, 2013.

Touching Distance
Martin Hardy

The Manager
Ron Atkinson

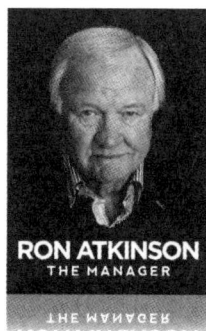

Up There
Michael Walker

The Unbelievables
David Bevan

Love Affairs & Marriage
Howard Kendall

When Friday Comes
James Montague

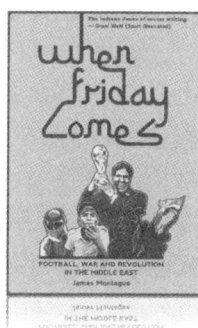

61 Minutes in Munich
Howard Gayle

The Acid Test
Clyde Best

The Binman Chronicles
Neville Southall